The Catholic Old Testament

A Beginner's Guide

CinderPress Beliefs Publishing

Table of Contents

Chapter 1: Introduction to the Old Testament

Welcome to a journey through the sacred and storied pages of the Old Testament, a literary treasure trove that forms the foundation of the Catholic faith. This chapter, "Introduction to the Old Testament," marks the beginning of your exploration into the rich tapestry of texts, narratives, and teachings that make up this ancient and revered collection. The Old Testament, often referred to as the Hebrew Bible, is a testament to the enduring relationship between God and humanity. In this introductory chapter, we set the stage for our adventure by peeling back the layers of history, culture, and spirituality that enshroud the Old Testament.

To fully grasp the Old Testament's significance, it's essential to embark on a journey through time. We'll delve into the origins, composition, and evolution of these sacred scriptures. Understanding the historical context in which these texts emerged provides invaluable insights into the messages they convey and their enduring impact on faith and culture. For Catholics, the Old Testament is more than a historical artifact; it's a living testament to the faith's roots and foundational beliefs. This chapter will illuminate the Old Testament's profound role within the Catholic tradition, illustrating how it weaves through the fabric of Catholic worship, theology, and spirituality.

The Old Testament is a diverse collection of books, each with its own style, genre, and message. As we navigate its pages, we'll categorize these texts, from epic narratives to prophetic revelations, and explore their unique contributions to the Old Testament's rich mosaic. This diversity offers a comprehensive view of God's relationship with humanity throughout history. Whether you're new to the Old Testament or seeking to deepen your understanding, "The Catholic Old Testament: A Beginner's Guide" is tailored for you. It serves as a beacon of knowledge, illuminating the Old Testament's timeless wisdom and its relevance to contemporary life and faith.

The Old Testament is a source of inspiration, moral guidance, and spiritual reflection. As we embark on this journey together, let's unlock the treasures hidden within its verses, explore its profound narratives, and discover the enduring messages that continue to resonate in the hearts and minds of believers.

The Importance of the Old Testament in Catholic Faith

The Old Testament holds a central and indispensable role within the Catholic faith, serving as a rich source of theological, moral, and spiritual guidance. For Catholics, it is not merely an ancient collection of texts but a living testament to God's revelation and the foundational narratives of their religious tradition. In this section, we delve into the profound importance of the Old Testament in Catholic faith.

1. Roots of the Faith

The Old Testament provides the historical and theological roots of the Catholic faith. It offers a detailed account of God's covenant with humanity, beginning with the patriarchs like Abraham and continuing through the formation of the Israelite nation. These foundational stories establish the divine relationship that culminates in the New Testament with the coming of Jesus Christ.

2. Divine Revelation

Catholics believe that the Old Testament, like the New Testament, is a vehicle of divine revelation. It contains God's self-disclosure, His character, His will for humanity, and His ethical and moral standards. The Ten Commandments, given to Moses on Mount Sinai, are one of the most iconic examples of divine revelation in the Old Testament, guiding Catholic ethical and moral principles.

3. Liturgical Use

The Old Testament plays a prominent role in the liturgical life of the Catholic Church. Numerous psalms, prayers, and readings are drawn from the Old Testament, enriching the liturgical experience. The Psalms, for instance, are frequently recited in Catholic worship, reflecting themes of praise, supplication, and lament.

4. Prefiguration of Christ

Catholics believe that the Old Testament contains foreshadowings or "types" of Christ, which find their fulfillment in the New Testament. These typological connections underscore the unity of God's plan throughout salvation history. For example, the paschal lamb of the Exodus prefigures Jesus as the "Lamb of God" in Christian theology.

5. Moral and Ethical Guidance

The Old Testament offers profound moral and ethical guidance for Catholics. The narratives, commandments, and wisdom literature found within its pages provide a framework for virtuous living. The Book of Proverbs, for instance, imparts practical wisdom, while the stories of figures like Joseph and Daniel exemplify ethical integrity in the face of adversity.

6. Inspiration for Compassion and Justice

The Old Testament frequently emphasizes the importance of compassion, justice, and care for the vulnerable. It calls upon Catholics to emulate these virtues in their daily lives. The prophets, such as Isaiah and Amos, passionately advocate for social justice, inspiring Catholics to work for the welfare of others and the common good.

7. Sacred Tradition

In Catholic theology, sacred tradition—alongside sacred Scripture—is a source of divine revelation. The Old Testament forms an integral part of this sacred tradition, passed down through the Church's teaching, liturgy, and interpretation. It shapes the Church's beliefs, doctrines, and moral teachings.

8. A Living Word

The Old Testament is not a relic of the past but a living word that continues to inspire and guide Catholics in their faith journey. Its narratives, poetry, and teachings resonate with the human experience, offering timeless insights into the nature of God and humanity.

The Old Testament occupies a paramount position in Catholic faith, serving as the foundational text that informs belief, worship, and ethical conduct. Its narratives, teachings, and enduring relevance underscore its indispensable role in shaping the Catholic tradition and the spiritual lives of millions of believers.

Overview of the Old Testament Books

The Old Testament, a collection of ancient texts that span centuries and encompass various genres, is the cornerstone of the Catholic faith. Its diverse books provide a multifaceted understanding of God's relationship with humanity, the moral and ethical principles of living, and the unfolding narrative of salvation history.

The Old Testament is traditionally divided into several categories, each with a unique focus and literary style. Understanding these categories helps readers navigate the richness of the Old Testament's content:

> **Historical Books:** These books recount the history of the Israelite people, from their early days in the Promised Land to their periods of exile and return. Notable books include Joshua, Judges, Samuel, and Kings.
>
> **Pentateuch:** Also known as the Torah, the Pentateuch consists of the first five books of the Old Testament: Genesis, Exodus, Leviticus, Numbers, and

Deuteronomy. It contains the foundational stories of creation, the patriarchs, and the Mosaic Law.

Wisdom Literature: Wisdom books such as Job, Proverbs, Ecclesiastes, Wisdom, and Sirach (Ecclesiasticus) offer practical guidance for virtuous living and explore the complexities of human existence.

Prophetic Books: The prophetic books, divided into major prophets (e.g., Isaiah, Jeremiah, Ezekiel) and minor prophets (e.g., Hosea, Amos, Micah), contain messages of divine judgment, repentance, and the promise of a future Messiah.

Psalms and Poetry: The Book of Psalms is a collection of religious poetry and songs that express a wide range of human emotions, from praise and thanksgiving to lament and supplication.

Apocalyptic Literature: Found in texts like Daniel and portions of Ezekiel and Zechariah, apocalyptic literature uses vivid symbolism and imagery to convey messages about divine judgment, eschatological hope, and the triumph of God's kingdom.

Key Old Testament Books

Within these categories, certain Old Testament books stand out for their theological significance and enduring impact:

Genesis: The book of beginnings, Genesis narrates the creation of the world, the stories of the patriarchs, and the origins of the Israelite people. It introduces themes of covenant, faith, and God's providence.

Exodus: Exodus recounts the epic story of the Israelites' liberation from slavery in Egypt and the giving of the Mosaic Law, including the Ten Commandments.

Psalms: The Psalms offer a diverse collection of prayers and hymns that express the full range of human emotions and serve as a resource for worship and reflection.

Isaiah: The book of Isaiah contains prophecies about the Messiah and themes of redemption and restoration, making it particularly significant for Christians.

Proverbs: Proverbs imparts practical wisdom for daily living, addressing ethical and moral principles that guide virtuous behavior.

Jeremiah: Jeremiah's prophetic messages emphasize repentance and God's faithfulness, even in times of exile and suffering.

The Old Testament, with its diverse genres and themes, weaves a comprehensive tapestry of religious thought, history, and spirituality. These books collectively contribute to the foundational understanding of God's relationship with humanity, the moral principles that guide life, and the promises of redemption that find their fulfillment in the New Testament.

How the Old Testament Differs from the New Testament

The Old Testament and the New Testament, both integral to the Christian faith, are distinct collections of texts with unique characteristics and purposes. Understanding the differences between them is essential for gaining a comprehensive grasp of the Catholic faith.

1. Covenant and Era

One of the fundamental differences between the Old and New Testaments lies in the era they represent and the covenants they emphasize:

- Old Testament: The Old Testament primarily focuses on the covenant between God and the people of Israel, established through figures like Abraham and Moses. It details the history of Israel, the Mosaic Law, and God's interactions with His chosen people.
- New Testament: The New Testament introduces a new covenant, centered on the person of Jesus Christ. It marks the beginning of a new era in God's relationship

with humanity, emphasizing grace, forgiveness, and salvation through faith in Jesus.

2. Fulfillment and Prophecy

The New Testament is often seen as the fulfillment of the promises and prophecies found in the Old Testament:

- Old Testament: The Old Testament contains numerous prophecies and types that anticipate the coming of the Messiah, the "Anointed One." These prophetic texts lay the foundation for the Messianic expectations of the Jewish people.
- New Testament: The New Testament reveals Jesus as the long-awaited Messiah, fulfilling the Old Testament prophecies. The Gospels present Jesus as the fulfillment of the Law and the Prophets, embodying the promises made to Israel.

3. Theology and Revelation

While both Testaments convey theological truths, they do so with different emphases:

- Old Testament: The Old Testament primarily reveals God's character, His sovereignty, and His covenantal relationship with humanity. It explores themes of creation, sin, and the need for redemption but often leaves these concepts open-ended, awaiting fulfillment.
- New Testament: The New Testament provides a clearer understanding of God's plan for salvation through Jesus Christ. It reveals the mystery of the Incarnation, the significance of the Cross and Resurrection, and the theological foundations of Christianity, including the doctrine of the Trinity.

4. Ethical Emphasis

The Old and New Testaments also differ in their ethical teachings and emphasis:

- Old Testament: The Old Testament contains the moral code of the Mosaic Law, encapsulated in the Ten Commandments and other legal statutes. It emphasizes obedience to these laws as a means of righteousness.
- New Testament: The New Testament shifts the emphasis from external observance to inner transformation through faith in Christ. It underscores love, grace, and the indwelling of the Holy Spirit as central to Christian ethics.

5. Language and Cultural Context

The Old and New Testaments were written in different languages and within distinct cultural contexts:

- Old Testament: The Old Testament was mainly composed in Hebrew, with some portions in Aramaic. It reflects the cultural and historical milieu of ancient Israel and its surrounding regions.
- New Testament: The New Testament was written in Greek, reflecting the Hellenistic culture of the Eastern Mediterranean. It emerged in a world influenced by Roman rule and Greek philosophy.

6. Composition and Literary Styles

The Old and New Testaments exhibit diverse literary styles and genres:

- Old Testament: The Old Testament includes historical narratives, poetry (e.g., Psalms), prophecy, wisdom literature (e.g., Proverbs), and legal codes. It features complex narratives with multiple authors.
- New Testament: The New Testament encompasses the Gospels (biographical accounts of Jesus' life), epistles (letters), apocalyptic literature (e.g., Revelation), and Acts of the Apostles. It focuses on the life, teachings, and impact of Jesus, as well as the early Christian communities.

Chapter 2: Understanding the Old Testament

"Understanding the Old Testament," the second chapter of our book, invites you to delve deeper into this sacred text. It equips you with the knowledge and tools needed to navigate the Old Testament's multifaceted landscape and discover the profound messages it holds for believers and seekers alike. This chapter will guide you through the layers of meaning, the historical contexts, and the theological insights that enrich the Old Testament's timeless pages.

One of the essential aspects of understanding the Old Testament is interpretation. It has been studied, debated, and cherished for centuries, and its texts are open to a range of interpretations. In this chapter, we will explore different methods of interpreting the Old Testament, including historical-critical, literary, and theological approaches. These perspectives offer diverse insights that deepen our understanding of the Old Testament's significance.

The Old Testament lays the theological foundation for much of Catholic doctrine. It introduces key concepts like covenant, sin, redemption, and God's providence, all of which find their fulfillment in the New Testament. By understanding the theological significance of the Old Testament, we gain a more profound appreciation of how it shapes Catholic beliefs and practices.

To truly understand the Old Testament, we must immerse ourselves in the historical and cultural context of ancient Israel. This chapter will take you back in time to the world of the Israelites, exploring their customs, traditions, and the challenges they faced. This context provides valuable insights into the motivations, hopes, and struggles of the people whose stories are preserved in these sacred texts.

The Old Testament is not a relic of the past but a living, relevant source of inspiration for contemporary life. Its stories, teachings, and wisdom continue to resonate with themes of faith, justice, and human experience. It is a source of enduring wisdom and guidance, and it holds the potential to enrich your faith and spiritual journey.

Historical and Cultural Context

To truly understand the Old Testament and the narratives it contains, one must step back in time to the world of ancient Israel. This section immerses you in the rich tapestry of history, culture, and society that shaped the lives of the people whose stories are preserved in these sacred texts.

Ancient Israel: The Setting of the Old Testament

Geography: The land of ancient Israel, situated in the eastern Mediterranean, played a pivotal role in the Old Testament's narratives. Understanding its diverse geography—ranging from the coastal plains to the arid wilderness and mountainous terrain—provides insights into the experiences of its inhabitants.

Key Locations in the Old testament includes:

- Mesopotamia: Mesopotamia, often referred to as the "land between the rivers," is located between the Tigris and Euphrates rivers. It includes regions like Sumer, Akkad, and Babylon, where early events in the Old Testament, such as the story of Abraham, took place.
- Canaan: Canaan is the Promised Land where the Israelites settled. It is located in the eastern Mediterranean region, encompassing modern-day Israel, Palestine, and parts of Jordan, Lebanon, and Syria.
- Egypt: Egypt is located to the southwest of Canaan, along the Nile River. It plays a significant role in the Old Testament, particularly in the stories of Joseph, Moses, and the Exodus.

- Mount Sinai: Mount Sinai is traditionally associated with the location where Moses received the Ten Commandments. Its exact location remains uncertain, but it is generally believed to be in the southern part of the Sinai Peninsula.

- Babylon: Babylon, located in ancient Mesopotamia, was a major city-state in the Old Testament and features prominently in the stories of the Babylonian Exile and the Book of Daniel.

- Nineveh: Nineveh was the capital of the Assyrian Empire and is mentioned in the Book of Jonah. It was situated on the eastern bank of the Tigris River, in modern-day Iraq.

- Jerusalem: Jerusalem, the capital of ancient Israel, is a central location in the Old Testament. It is situated in the central highlands of Canaan and remains a significant city in modern Israel.

- Bethlehem: Bethlehem, a town in Judah, is the birthplace of King David and, according to the New Testament, Jesus. It is located near Jerusalem.

- Jericho: Jericho is one of the oldest inhabited cities in the world and is mentioned in the Old Testament as the site of Joshua's famous victory when the walls of the city fell.

- Red Sea: The Red Sea is the body of water that the Israelites crossed during the Exodus, according to the Old Testament.

- Jordan River: The Jordan River flows through the region, forming part of the eastern border of Canaan. It plays a crucial role in several Old Testament stories, including the crossing into the Promised Land.

Historical Timeline: The Old Testament covers a vast span of time, from the earliest creation stories to the Babylonian exile and beyond. (See Appendix B)

Cultural and Religious Practices

Covenant and Religion: The concept of covenant, a binding agreement between God and humanity, forms the theological foundation of the Old Testament. Covenants and religious practices held immense significance in the lives of the ancient Israelites. These elements were central to their relationship with God, their identity as a chosen people, and their expression of faith.

The Significance of Covenants:

Covenant is a recurring theme in the Old Testament. It represents a sacred agreement or contract between God and His people. Several key covenants shaped the course of Israelite history:

- The Abrahamic Covenant: This covenant, established with Abraham, promised him numerous descendants and a land, which became the foundation for the people of Israel. It symbolizes God's enduring promise to His chosen people.
- The Mosaic Covenant: The covenant at Mount Sinai, mediated by Moses, included the Ten Commandments and a complex system of laws. It governed every aspect of the Israelites' lives, emphasizing righteousness, justice, and holiness.
- The Davidic Covenant: God made a covenant with King David, promising that his lineage would produce an everlasting king. This covenant connects the messianic hope in the Old Testament to the coming of Jesus Christ in the New Testament.

These covenants served as the framework for the Israelites' relationship with God, shaping their moral and religious identity. They were not merely legal contracts but expressions of divine love and fidelity.

The Central Role of Religious Practices:

Religious practices were integral to the Israelite way of life. These practices encompassed rituals, sacrifices, and festivals, each with its own significance:

- Sacrifices: Offerings and sacrifices were central acts of worship. The burnt offering symbolized complete devotion, the sin offering sought forgiveness, and the peace offering fostered communion with God. The Passover lamb, in particular, commemorated the Israelites' liberation from Egypt.

- Rituals: Ritual purity was essential for approaching God. Rituals included circumcision as a sign of the covenant, the anointing of priests, and purification rites. The Day of Atonement, or Yom Kippur, was the most solemn ritual for seeking forgiveness of sins.

- Festivals: Festivals played a crucial role in Israelite religious life. Passover, Pentecost, and the Feast of Tabernacles were among the most significant. These festivals celebrated historical events, agricultural cycles, and the giving of the Law at Sinai.

Religious practices reinforced the Israelites' relationship with God, providing a means of atonement, thanksgiving, and communal unity. They also foreshadowed the coming of Christ, who fulfilled and transcended these rituals through His sacrifice on the cross.

Society and Social Structure: Examining the societal structure of ancient Israel, from tribal communities to the monarchy, reveals the dynamics of power, governance, and social responsibility. It also sheds light on the roles of prophets, judges, and kings in shaping the nation's destiny.

Tribal Communities and the Patriarchs:

At the outset of Israel's history, the people were organized into tribal communities. These tribes traced their lineage back to the twelve sons of Jacob, who was also known as Israel. The tribal structure defined early Israelite society and played a significant role in shaping its identity.

- Patriarchs: The patriarchs, including Abraham, Isaac, and Jacob, were revered figures who received divine promises and covenants from God. These promises formed the foundation of Israel's identity as a chosen people.

- Tribal Leaders: Within each tribe, leaders emerged as judges and arbiters of disputes. These leaders played vital roles in maintaining order and justice in their respective communities.

The Exodus and the Wilderness Journey:

The Exodus from Egypt marked a pivotal moment in Israel's history. Led by Moses, the Israelites journeyed through the wilderness, forging their identity as a people and receiving the divine law at Mount Sinai.

- Moses and the Prophets: Moses, a prophet and leader, communicated directly with God and guided the Israelites through the wilderness. His role exemplified the prophetic tradition, which would continue throughout Israel's history.

The Period of Judges:

Following the wilderness journey, the Israelites settled in Canaan. During this time, the nation was characterized by a loose confederation of tribes and a lack of centralized leadership.

- Judges: Judges were charismatic leaders raised by God to deliver the Israelites from oppressors, such as the Canaanites. These figures, like Deborah and Samson, played pivotal roles in times of crisis.

The Monarchic Era:

Israel's transition to a monarchy marked a significant shift in its societal structure.

- Kings and Prophets: Prophets, such as Samuel and Nathan, emerged as key figures in the courts of kings. They served as advisors, counselors, and messengers of God, often challenging kings to uphold God's covenant.

- David and Solomon: King David and his son Solomon established a centralized monarchy, with Jerusalem as the capital. David's covenant with God and Solomon's wisdom defined this era.

Division and Exile:

The kingdom divided into the northern kingdom of Israel and the southern kingdom of Judah following Solomon's rule. This division led to complex dynamics of power, idolatry, and foreign influence.

- Prophets as Reformers: Prophets like Elijah, Isaiah, and Jeremiah emerged as powerful voices during these turbulent times. They called for repentance, social justice, and fidelity to the covenant.

Law and Justice: The Old Testament includes the Mosaic Law, a comprehensive legal code that governed various aspects of life, from worship to civil matters. The Mosaic Law, often referred to as the Law of Moses or the Torah, occupies a central place in the Old Testament and is a foundational aspect of Israelite ethics and religious practice.

Origins and Significance:
Divine Revelation: The Mosaic Law is attributed to Moses, who received it directly from God during the Israelites' sojourn in the wilderness. It is considered a divine revelation and covenant between God and His chosen people.
Moral and Legal Framework: The Law of Moses provided a comprehensive moral and legal framework for the Israelites. It encompassed religious rituals, ethical guidelines, social justice, and civil laws, establishing a holistic way of life.

Components of the Mosaic Law:

The Ten Commandments: At the heart of the Mosaic Law are the Ten Commandments, a concise and profound set of ethical principles that emphasize love of God and love of neighbor. They are foundational to Catholic moral teaching.

Ceremonial and Sacrificial Laws: The Mosaic Law included detailed instructions for religious rituals, including the construction and service of the Tabernacle, the priesthood, and various sacrificial offerings. These rituals foreshadowed the ultimate sacrifice of Jesus Christ.

Civil and Social Laws: The law addressed matters of social justice, such as laws concerning property, justice, and community welfare. It promoted fairness and compassion within the community.

Challenges and Renewal:

Challenges in Observance: Throughout the Old Testament, there are accounts of the Israelites struggling to fully observe the Mosaic Law. The prophets often called the people to return to fidelity to the covenant.

Renewal and Interpretation: The Mosaic Law has been subject to interpretation and renewal over the centuries. Jewish scholars, rabbis, and theologians have provided insights and commentary, shaping its application in different historical contexts.

Catholic Perspective:

Continuity and Fulfillment: The Catholic Church recognizes the continuity between the Old and New Testaments. While the ceremonial and sacrificial aspects of the Mosaic Law have been fulfilled in Christ, the moral principles and ethical teachings remain relevant.

Guidance for Christian Life: The moral principles of the Mosaic Law, particularly the Ten Commandments, serve as a guide for Christian ethical living. They underscore the importance of love, justice, and reverence for God.

Connection to the Eucharist: The Catholic Mass, particularly the Eucharistic sacrifice, draws on elements of the Mosaic sacrificial system. The Eucharist is seen as the ultimate fulfillment of these sacrifices.

Cultural and Literary Traditions

Oral Tradition: Before being written down, many Old Testament stories were part of an oral tradition, passed down through generations. Oral storytelling played a pivotal role in preserving the narratives and themes of the Old Testament, ensuring that these sacred stories were passed down through generations.

The Power of Oral Tradition:

Ancient Origins: Long before the Old Testament texts were written, the stories, genealogies, and teachings of the Israelite people were transmitted orally from one generation to the next. This oral tradition was the primary means of preserving cultural and religious heritage.

Accessibility: The oral tradition made these narratives accessible to all, regardless of literacy. People of various backgrounds and ages could participate in the retelling and transmission of these stories, reinforcing a sense of communal identity.

Preserving the Covenant Story:

Passing Down the Covenant: Central to the Old Testament is the covenant between God and the Israelites. The stories of God's promises, commandments, and the people's response were faithfully passed down through oral tradition.

Deepening Faith: Oral storytelling allowed for a dynamic and interactive engagement with these narratives. Listeners could ask questions, discuss interpretations, and immerse themselves in the spiritual and moral lessons embedded in the stories.

Narrative Themes and Lessons:

Moral and Ethical Guidance: The oral tradition conveyed moral and ethical principles that guided the lives of the Israelites. Stories of virtue, faith, and the consequences of disobedience served as teaching tools.

Identity and Communal Unity: The stories of the patriarchs, the Exodus, and the judges reinforced the Israelites' identity as a chosen people. This collective memory fostered a strong sense of communal unity and purpose.

Transition to Written Texts:

Recording the Tradition: Over time, some of these oral traditions were transcribed into written texts, preserving them for future generations. These written records, which became books of the Old Testament, were a continuation of the oral storytelling tradition.

Interplay with Written Texts: Even as written texts emerged, oral storytelling continued to complement and enrich the understanding of the Old Testament. Public recitations of scripture and oral retellings of biblical stories remained integral to religious practice.

Literary Genres: The Old Testament encompasses diverse literary genres, from historical narratives to poetry, prophecy, and wisdom literature. (See Chapter 2: Literary Styles in the Old Testament)

Neighbor Nations and Influences

Interaction with Neighboring Cultures: Ancient Israel interacted with neighboring nations such as Egypt, Mesopotamia, and Canaan, which influenced its culture, language, and religious practices. Ancient Israel's interactions with neighboring cultures left a significant imprint on the Old Testament, shaping its narratives, theology, and cultural context.

1. Egyptian Influence:

- Exodus and the Egyptian Experience: The Israelites' captivity in Egypt and their subsequent Exodus played a foundational role in Israel's identity. The stories of Moses, the plagues, and the Passover were deeply influenced by the Egyptian context.
- Monotheism and Henotheism: Egypt's religious landscape, characterized by polytheism and henotheism (the worship of one god without denying the existence of others), likely influenced Israel's early understanding of monotheism.

2. Canaanite Influence:

- Canaanite Deities and Worship: The Canaanites, who inhabited the Promised Land, worshiped a pantheon of gods and goddesses. Israel's interactions with the Canaanites raised theological challenges and moral dilemmas, as seen in the Old Testament's emphasis on monotheism and the rejection of idolatry.
- Incorporation and Confrontation: Israel sometimes incorporated elements of Canaanite culture and religion, such as place names and agricultural practices. However, the Old Testament also contains narratives of confrontation with Canaanite practices, particularly in the prophetic literature.

3. Mesopotamian and Babylonian Influence:

- Babylonian Exile: The Babylonian Exile in the 6th century BCE had a profound impact on Israelite theology and literature. It prompted reflection on issues of suffering, exile, and the covenant. The Book of Daniel, for example, reflects elements of Babylonian wisdom literature.
- Cultural Exchange: During the exile, there was a cultural exchange between the Israelites and the Babylonians, which influenced the development of apocalyptic literature and eschatological thinking in the Old Testament.

4. Persian Influence:

- Return from Exile: The Persian Empire's conquest of Babylon allowed for the return of Israelites to their homeland. This period is marked by the books of Ezra and Nehemiah, which detail the restoration of Jerusalem and the reestablishment of religious practices.

5. Assyrian Influence:

- Assyrian Threat and Exile: The Assyrian Empire's invasion of the northern kingdom of Israel in the 8th century BCE resulted in the exile of the ten northern tribes. This event influenced the prophetic literature and the development of Israelite identity.

Impact on the Old Testament:

- Theological Reflection: Israel's encounters with neighboring cultures led to theological reflection on issues of identity, monotheism, idolatry, and the covenant, which are evident throughout the Old Testament.
- Literary Adaptation: The Old Testament reflects the literary adaptation of Israelite traditions and stories to engage with the theological challenges posed by neighboring cultures. This adaptation allowed Israel to affirm its unique identity and relationship with God.
- Continuity and Renewal: While influenced by neighboring cultures, the Old Testament also emphasizes continuity with the Abrahamic covenant and renewal of faithfulness to God.

Babylonian Exile: The Babylonian exile was a pivotal period in Israel's history. The exile and its aftermath stand as a crucible of faith in the Old Testament, revealing profound themes of hope, restoration, and spiritual reflection.

A Period of Desolation:

The Exile's Impact: The Babylonian Exile was a period of desolation, marked by the destruction of Jerusalem and the Temple, forced deportation, and a sense of profound loss. The Israelites were confronted with the consequences of their unfaithfulness to God's covenant.

Themes of Hope:

Divine Promises: Amid the despair, prophets like Jeremiah and Ezekiel emerged as bearers of hope. They delivered messages of God's enduring love and promises of restoration. These prophetic voices illuminated the path toward hope in the midst of adversity.

The Return of the Exiles: The decree of Cyrus the Great of Persia, allowing the exiles to return to their homeland and rebuild the Temple, became a beacon of hope. This return marked the beginning of a new chapter in Israel's history.

Themes of Restoration:

Rebuilding Jerusalem: The books of Ezra and Nehemiah vividly recount the efforts to rebuild Jerusalem's walls and restore the city's spiritual and physical infrastructure. These narratives underscore the importance of restoration after a period of devastation.

The Renewed Covenant: The exile prompted a renewed commitment to the covenant with God. The people rededicated themselves to following God's commandments, as reflected in the post-exilic books of the Old Testament.

Spiritual Reflection and Renewal:

Lamentations: The Book of Lamentations captures the deep sorrow and lamentation of the exiled community. It serves as a powerful expression of human suffering and the need for spiritual reflection.

Prophetic Witness: The prophetic literature during the exile emphasized the importance of spiritual reflection and repentance. It called the people to examine their ways and turn back to God.

Legacy and Spiritual Insights:

Theological Growth: The Babylonian Exile and its aftermath contributed to significant theological growth within the Old Testament. The experience deepened the understanding of divine justice, covenant faithfulness, and the enduring love of God.

Themes of Resurrection: The hope and restoration witnessed during and after the exile laid the groundwork for later theological concepts, including those related to resurrection, eschatology, and the enduring faithfulness of God.

By delving into the historical and cultural context of the Old Testament, we gain a deeper appreciation of its narratives, teachings, and themes. This context provides a lens through which we can interpret the motivations, struggles, and aspirations of the people whose stories are intertwined with the divine. Moreover, it underscores the enduring relevance of the Old Testament, which continues to resonate with contemporary discussions on faith, justice, morality, and human experience.

Literary Styles in the Old Testament

The Old Testament is a rich tapestry of literary styles and genres that encompass historical narratives, poetry, prophecy, wisdom literature, and legal codes. These diverse forms of expression enhance the depth and breadth of the Old Testament's messages, making it a captivating and multifaceted collection.

Narrative Prose

Historical Narratives: The Old Testament contains historical narratives that recount the foundational events and figures of Israel's history. Books like Genesis, Exodus, Joshua, and Kings provide a narrative framework for understanding God's relationship with His people and the unfolding of His divine plan.

Poetry and Song

The Psalms: Perhaps the most famous poetic section of the Old Testament, the Book of Psalms is a collection of 150 poetic songs and prayers. These psalms encompass a wide range of emotions, from praise and thanksgiving to lament and supplication, making them a source of solace, inspiration, and devotion in both Jewish and Christian worship.

Song of Songs: This poetic book celebrates the beauty of love and desire, using vivid and sensual imagery. It is traditionally understood as an allegory of the divine love between God and His people.

Prophecy

Prophetic Oracles: The prophetic books, including Isaiah, Jeremiah, and Ezekiel, feature messages from God delivered through prophets. These oracles often convey divine judgment, calls to repentance, and promises of restoration, offering insight into the spiritual and moral condition of Israel.

Wisdom Literature

Proverbs: The Book of Proverbs imparts practical wisdom for daily living. It consists of short, pithy sayings that offer guidance on a wide range of topics, from ethics and morality to practical advice for successful living.

Ecclesiastes: Ecclesiastes explores the meaning of life and the human condition. It contains philosophical reflections on the futility of worldly pursuits and the search for true wisdom.

Legal Codes

The Mosaic Law: The books of Exodus, Leviticus, Numbers, and Deuteronomy contain legal codes and regulations that governed various aspects of ancient Israelite life, including religious worship, ethical conduct, and civil matters. These laws reflect the covenantal relationship between God and Israel.

Prophetic and Apocalyptic Literature

Prophetic Vision: Some prophetic books, like Daniel and portions of Ezekiel and Zechariah, incorporate vivid and symbolic imagery to convey messages about divine judgment, eschatological hope, and the triumph of God's kingdom.

Parables and Allegories

Parables: While parables are more commonly associated with the New Testament, the Old Testament also contains stories with moral or allegorical significance. For example, the story of Nathan's parable to King David serves as a powerful indictment of sin and repentance (2 Samuel 12:1-14).

Interplay of Literary Styles

The Old Testament's beauty lies in the interplay of these literary styles. Narratives are interspersed with poetic expressions, prophetic oracles, and wisdom sayings, creating a mosaic of meaning that invites readers to engage with its messages on multiple levels.

Understanding the diverse literary styles of the Old Testament enhances our appreciation of the texts' unique qualities and purposes. It allows us to approach the Old Testament with a deeper awareness of the literary techniques employed by its authors, and it enriches our comprehension of the timeless truths and wisdom contained within its pages.

Key Themes and Messages

The Old Testament is a treasure trove of timeless themes and profound messages that continue to resonate with believers and seekers alike.

1. Covenant and Relationship with God

At the heart of the Old Testament is the theme of covenant—a binding agreement between God and His people. The covenantal relationship is central to understanding God's commitment to humanity and humanity's responsibility to live in accordance with God's commands. Key covenants, such as those with Noah, Abraham, Moses, and David, emphasize God's faithfulness, love, and desire for a faithful response from His people.

2. Creation and the Divine Order

The Old Testament opens with the majestic account of creation in the book of Genesis. This narrative highlights the goodness of God's creation, the dignity of humanity as bearers of His image, and the responsibility to care for the earth. It underscores the foundational belief that God is the Creator and Sustainer of all life.

3. The Problem of Sin and Redemption

The Old Testament addresses the human condition, including the presence of sin and its consequences. Stories of disobedience, exile, and suffering reveal the profound impact of sin on individuals and communities. However, the Old Testament also offers a message of hope and redemption, emphasizing God's mercy and His desire to restore humanity to a right relationship with Him.

4. God's Providence and Guidance

Throughout the Old Testament, we see God's providential care and guidance for His people. The Exodus narrative, with its liberation from slavery and guidance through the wilderness, exemplifies God's providence. These stories remind us that God is actively involved in human history and leads His people on a journey of faith.

5. Justice and Compassion

The Old Testament places a strong emphasis on justice and compassion, urging God's people to care for the vulnerable and seek social justice. Prophets like Isaiah and Amos passionately advocate for the rights of the poor and marginalized, highlighting the importance of ethical living and societal responsibility.

6. Messianic Expectations

Throughout the Old Testament, we encounter prophecies and types that point to the coming of a Messiah—a savior figure who will bring salvation and fulfill God's promises. These Messianic expectations find their fulfillment in the New Testament with the arrival of Jesus Christ.

7. Wisdom for Life

The Old Testament contains a wealth of wisdom literature, including the Book of Proverbs and Ecclesiastes. These texts offer practical guidance for virtuous living, ethical decision-making, and the pursuit of wisdom. They provide timeless insights into the complexities of human existence.

8. Faith and Obedience

Many Old Testament figures, such as Abraham, Moses, and the prophets, exemplify faith and obedience to God's call. Their stories serve as models of trust and fidelity, encouraging readers to respond to God's invitations with unwavering faith.

9. Divine Revelation

The Old Testament serves as a vehicle of divine revelation, containing God's self-disclosure, His character, His will for humanity, and His ethical and moral standards. It provides a foundational understanding of God's attributes and His relationship with humanity.

10. Hope and Restoration

Despite trials and tribulations, the Old Testament instills hope in the promise of restoration and God's ultimate triumph over evil. The prophetic messages of hope, such as those found in Isaiah and Jeremiah, anticipate a future of renewal and redemption.

These key themes and messages interweave throughout the Old Testament, forming a cohesive narrative that offers profound insights into the human experience, the nature of God, and the ethical principles that guide life. As we explore the Old Testament's narratives and teachings, we uncover the enduring wisdom and spiritual guidance it offers to readers of all backgrounds and walks of life.

Chapter 3: Genesis - The Beginning of Creation

In the pages of the Old Testament, the book of Genesis stands as a majestic prologue—an introduction to the grand narrative of creation, humanity's origins, and God's enduring relationship with His creation. Genesis serves as the foundational text for numerous aspects of faith and theology. It unfolds the story of creation, the emergence of humanity, and the beginnings of God's covenantal relationship with His people. As we explore the narrative of Genesis, we delve into the core beliefs that underpin the Catholic faith and Christian theology.

Genesis is not only about the creation of the world but also the call of individuals who would play pivotal roles in God's plan. The calling of Abraham, a central figure in Genesis, marks the beginning of God's covenant with a chosen people. His journey of faith serves as an inspiring example of obedience and trust in God's promises. Genesis also introduces themes that reverberate throughout the Old and New Testaments—themes of faith, redemption, and the anticipation of a future Messiah.

The creation stories, the narratives of Adam and Eve, and the call of Abraham are more than ancient tales; they are living testimonies to God's enduring love and His invitation to enter into a covenantal relationship. These stories continue to inspire, challenge, and illuminate our understanding of God's creative power, His covenantal love, and the human journey of faith.

Creation Stories in Genesis

The opening chapters of the book of Genesis contain two distinct but complementary creation stories. These narratives are among the most renowned and profound in the entire Old Testament, and they offer essential insights into the Catholic faith's understanding of creation, the nature of God, and humanity's role in the world.

1. Creation Story in Genesis 1:1-2:3

Creation Ex Nihilo: The first creation account, found in Genesis 1:1-2:3, opens with the famous words, "In the beginning, God created the heavens and the earth." This story emphasizes the concept of creatio ex nihilo, the creation of the world from nothing by the divine Word. It unfolds a structured, six-day narrative of God's creative activity, culminating in the Sabbath, a day of rest and consecration.

The Order of Creation: Genesis 1 describes the systematic formation of the cosmos, including the separation of light from darkness, the creation of the heavens and the earth, the emergence of the seas, the formation of land, the appearance of vegetation, the creation of celestial bodies, the emergence of sea and land creatures, and, ultimately, the creation of humanity—male and female—in the divine image.

Human Dominion and Stewardship: This creation account bestows upon humanity the responsibility of stewardship over the earth and its creatures. Humans are created in God's image, and they are given dominion over creation while being entrusted with the task of caring for it.

2. Creation Story in Genesis 2:4-25

The Garden of Eden: The second creation account, beginning in Genesis 2:4, offers a more intimate and detailed perspective on the creation of humanity and the Garden of Eden. Here, we find the narrative of God forming Adam from the dust of the earth and breathing life into him. Adam is placed in the Garden, where he names the animals and experiences a deep sense of solitude.

The Creation of Eve: In response to Adam's solitude, God creates Eve from Adam's rib, signifying their profound unity and interdependence. This account emphasizes the complementary nature of male and female and the institution of marriage.

The Fall and Its Consequences: The Garden narrative also introduces the serpent, who tempts Adam and Eve to eat from the forbidden tree of the knowledge of good and evil. Their disobedience leads to the Fall, resulting in a rupture in their relationship with God, their expulsion from the Garden, and the introduction of suffering, toil, and mortality.

Interpreting the Creation Stories

The creation stories in Genesis have been interpreted in various ways throughout history, encompassing both literal and allegorical interpretations. They offer rich theological insights, including:

- The affirmation of God as the Creator and Sustainer of the universe.
- Humanity's special place in creation, created in God's image and entrusted with stewardship.
- The goodness of creation as a reflection of God's nature.
- The consequences of human sin and the need for redemption.

Understanding these creation stories enhances our grasp of Catholic theology, morality, and the relationship between God, humanity, and the natural world. They serve as a profound foundation for exploring the broader themes of faith, redemption, and God's providence that unfold throughout the Old and New Testaments.

Adam and Eve: The First Humans

The story of Adam and Eve, found in the book of Genesis, is one of the most iconic and profound narratives in the Old Testament. It serves as a foundational account of humanity's origins, the consequences of disobedience, and the enduring themes of redemption and God's covenantal love.

Creation of Adam and Eve

Adam's Formation: In the second creation account (Genesis 2:4-25), God forms Adam from the dust of the earth and breathes the breath of life into him. Adam, the first human, is thus created in the image and likeness of God, reflecting a special closeness to the Divine Creator.

Eve's Creation: After placing Adam in the Garden of Eden, God recognizes that it is not good for Adam to be alone. He creates Eve from Adam's rib, highlighting their profound unity and complementarity. The creation of Eve underscores the divine intention for human community and companionship.

Life in the Garden of Eden

The Garden of Delight: Adam and Eve are placed in the Garden of Eden, a paradise of abundance and beauty. They are entrusted with the task of tending the garden and enjoying its fruits, with one notable exception—the tree of the knowledge of good and evil, from which they are forbidden to eat.

The Temptation and Fall: The serpent, embodying evil, tempts Eve and Adam to eat from the forbidden tree, questioning God's command. Succumbing to this temptation, they disobey God's explicit instruction and partake of the fruit. This act of disobedience is known as the Fall.

Consequences of the Fall

Alienation from God: The Fall results in a rupture in Adam and Eve's relationship with God. They experience guilt, shame, and a sense of separation from the divine presence.

God banishes them from the Garden of Eden, signifying the consequences of their disobedience.

Human Suffering: The consequences of the Fall extend beyond Adam and Eve. Human beings inherit the effects of original sin, leading to suffering, toil, and mortality. The story of Adam and Eve explains the existence of sin and the need for redemption in the human condition.

The story of Adam and Eve is not solely a tale of disobedience and its consequences; it also foreshadows themes of redemption and hope:

Promise of a Savior: Even in the aftermath of the Fall, God offers a glimmer of hope. He promises a future Redeemer who will crush the serpent's head (Genesis 3:15). This promise anticipates the Messianic hope that finds fulfillment in Jesus Christ.

Clothed in God's Mercy: After their disobedience, God clothes Adam and Eve with garments made from animal skins, symbolizing His mercy and provision. This act foreshadows the redemption that will come through the sacrificial shedding of blood—an image of Christ's redemptive sacrifice.

The story of Adam and Eve holds profound theological significance within the Catholic faith. It addresses essential theological themes, including:

- The dignity of human beings created in God's image.
- The reality of sin, its consequences, and the need for redemption.
- The promise of a future Savior and the hope of salvation.
- The importance of obedience and free will in human moral decision-making.

Noah and the Flood

The story of Noah and the Flood, found in the book of Genesis, is one of the most iconic and enduring narratives in the Old Testament. It presents themes of divine judgment, human obedience, and God's covenantal promise. At the outset of the Flood narrative (Genesis 6:1-8), the text paints a grim picture of the state of humanity. Wickedness and corruption have spread throughout the world, and "the Lord saw that the wickedness of man was great in the earth and that every intention of the thoughts of his heart was only evil continually" (Genesis 6:5, ESV). Humanity's descent into sinfulness prompts God's decision to intervene.

Amid this backdrop of moral decay, Noah emerges as a figure of righteousness and obedience. God singles out Noah and his family for a specific purpose—to build an ark that will serve as a refuge from the impending floodwaters. Noah's faith and obedience to God's command stand in stark contrast to the prevailing wickedness. Noah, following God's instructions, undertakes the monumental task of constructing the ark. This massive vessel is to serve as a means of salvation for Noah, his family, and representatives of all land-dwelling creatures. The detailed description of the ark's design underscores the divine precision of God's plan.

As the floodwaters rise, they cover the entire earth, bringing about a cataclysmic event of unparalleled proportions. The flood lasts for 40 days and 40 nights, signifying a period of purification and renewal in biblical symbolism. All life on earth is submerged, except for those aboard the ark. After the floodwaters recede, God establishes a covenant with Noah—a covenant that extends to all of humanity. God promises never again to destroy the earth with a flood and sets the rainbow as a sign of this covenant (Genesis 9:8-17). This covenant underscores God's mercy, His commitment to the created order, and His invitation to humanity to participate in His divine plan.

The story of Noah and the Flood holds profound theological significance within the Catholic faith:

- *Divine Judgment and Mercy:* The Flood narrative illustrates the consequences of human sinfulness and God's judgment. However, it also highlights God's mercy in preserving a remnant through Noah.

- *Obedience and Righteousness:* Noah's obedience to God's command and his righteousness serve as models of faith and virtuous living.
- *Covenant and Promise:* The covenant established with Noah foreshadows God's future covenants with His people and underscores His faithfulness to His promises.
- *Renewal and Hope:* The Flood narrative offers a message of renewal and hope, symbolizing the possibility of redemption and a fresh start, even in the face of human sin.

The story of Noah and the Flood resonates with Catholic theology, emphasizing themes of obedience, covenant, mercy, and the transformative power of God's grace. It reminds believers of God's enduring commitment to humanity and His call to participate in His plan for salvation.

Chapter 4: Exodus - Liberation and the Covenant

In the tapestry of the Old Testament, few chapters resonate as powerfully as the story of Exodus. It is a tale of liberation, covenant, and divine guidance—a narrative that has left an indelible mark on the Catholic faith and the world's cultural and religious heritage. Exodus is also a story of spiritual transformation. The Israelites' journey through the wilderness becomes a metaphor for the human journey of faith—filled with trials, tests, and moments of divine guidance.

The Exodus narrative holds immense theological significance within the Catholic faith:

Divine Liberation: It underscores God's role as the liberator of His people, setting them free from bondage.

Covenant and Law: The covenant established at Mount Sinai forms the basis for the Mosaic Law, which guides the ethical and moral life of the Israelites and lays the foundation for Catholic moral teaching.

God's Guidance: Exodus reveals God's guidance and providence in the midst of life's challenges and uncertainties.

Redemption and Salvation: The Passover foreshadows the ultimate redemption and salvation that Christ will bring to humanity.

Moses and the Burning Bush

One of the most iconic and spiritually significant encounters in the Bible occurs in the book of Exodus when Moses encounters the burning bush. This event marks the beginning of Moses' mission as a liberator and leader of the Israelites.

Moses' life takes a dramatic turn when he encounters a burning bush in the wilderness of Mount Horeb, also known as Mount Sinai. The bush is burning but not consumed by the flames, a miraculous sight that captures Moses' attention. As he approaches the bush, he hears the voice of God calling him by name—"Moses, Moses!" In this sacred moment, God reveals His divine presence to Moses. He identifies Himself as the God of Abraham, Isaac, and Jacob—the God of the patriarchs. God speaks of the suffering of the Israelites in Egypt and expresses His concern for their plight. He declares His intention to rescue them from bondage and bring them to the land of Canaan, a "land flowing with milk and honey."

Moses, initially reluctant and overwhelmed by the gravity of the call, responds with uncertainty and self-doubt. He questions his qualifications and doubts whether the Israelites will believe him or listen to his message. In a profound dialogue with God, Moses seeks to understand God's identity and asks for a name to convey to the people. God responds with the sacred name "I AM WHO I AM," affirming His eternal and unchanging nature. God commissions Moses to go to Pharaoh, the ruler of Egypt, and demand the release of the Israelites. He equips Moses with miraculous signs and assures him that He will be with him throughout the mission. God also predicts Pharaoh's resistance but assures Moses of the ultimate victory that will result in the Israelites' liberation.

The encounter at the burning bush holds profound theological significance within the Catholic faith:

> *Divine Revelation:* The burning bush serves as a symbol of God's self-revelation to humanity, emphasizing His presence, holiness, and the sacredness of the moment.

> *The Call to Leadership:* Moses' call at the burning bush underscores the divine calling of leaders in salvation history. It becomes a model for responding to God's call with humility, trust, and obedience.

The Name "I AM WHO I AM": This sacred name signifies God's self-existence, His eternal nature, and His unchanging character. It emphasizes the divine mystery and majesty.

God's Compassion: God's concern for the suffering of the Israelites reveals His compassion and His desire to liberate the oppressed.

The story of Moses and the burning bush resonates with the Catholic faith's teachings on divine revelation, the call to mission and leadership, and the profound encounter with God's presence. It encourages believers to reflect on their own responses to God's call and the importance of trusting in His providence. Moses' journey from reluctance to obedience serves as an enduring inspiration for all who are called to serve God and His people. The burning bush remains a symbol of God's presence, guiding humanity through the wilderness of life and toward the Promised Land of eternal communion with Him.

The Exodus from Egypt

The Exodus from Egypt is a crucial event in the Old Testament, foundational to the identity and faith of the Israelite people. This dramatic story, recounted in the book of Exodus, marks their liberation from Egyptian slavery and the beginning of their journey toward the Promised Land.

The narrative of the Exodus begins with the Israelites living as slaves in Egypt. Under the oppressive rule of Pharaoh, they endure harsh labor and persecution. Their suffering and cries for deliverance reach the ears of God, who remembers His covenant with their ancestors. As we explored in a previous subchapter, Moses is called by God to lead the Israelites out of Egypt. This calling sets in motion a series of miraculous events and divine interventions that will culminate in their liberation.

God, through Moses and his brother Aaron, sends a series of ten plagues upon Egypt. These plagues are not only acts of divine judgment but also a demonstration of God's power and a challenge to Pharaoh's refusal to release the Israelites. The plagues include the turning of the Nile into blood, the infestation of frogs, gnats, flies, and locusts, the disease upon livestock, the boils and sores, the hailstorm and fire, the darkness, and, ultimately, the death of the firstborn. The most significant of these plagues is the death of the firstborn, which prompts Pharaoh to finally release the Israelites. Before their departure, God institutes the Passover as a memorial feast. The Israelites are instructed to mark their doorposts with the blood of a sacrificed lamb so that the angel of death will "pass over" their homes, sparing their firstborn sons.

With the tenth plague, Pharaoh relents, and the Israelites are freed from their bondage. This momentous event marks the beginning of their journey toward the Promised Land. The Israelites, numbering in the hundreds of thousands, depart from Egypt, carrying with them the spoils of their former masters. The Israelites' exodus leads them to the shores of the Red Sea, with Pharaoh and his army in pursuit. At this critical juncture, God miraculously parts the waters of the sea, allowing the Israelites to cross on dry ground. When Pharaoh's army attempts to follow, the waters return, drowning them and ensuring the Israelites' escape.

The Exodus from Egypt holds profound theological significance within the Catholic faith:

Liberation and Salvation: It symbolizes liberation from sin and slavery, foreshadowing the salvation that Christ would bring to humanity.

Divine Providence: The story underscores God's providential care for His people, guiding them through trials and difficulties.

The Passover: The Passover feast prefigures the Eucharist and Christ's sacrificial death, where His blood liberates believers from the bondage of sin.

Covenant Renewal: The Exodus leads to the renewal of God's covenant with the Israelites at Mount Sinai, a covenant that forms the basis of the Mosaic Law.

The Ten Commandments

The Ten Commandments, also known as the Decalogue, are a cornerstone of moral and ethical teachings within the Catholic faith. These divine instructions, given by God to Moses on Mount Sinai, are presented in the book of Exodus and are foundational to the Judeo-Christian tradition. The Ten Commandments are delivered to Moses as part of God's covenant with the Israelites at Mount Sinai. This divine encounter is marked by awe-inspiring manifestations of God's presence, including thunder, lightning, a thick cloud, and the sound of a trumpet (Exodus 19:16). The commandments are etched by the very finger of God onto stone tablets, symbolizing their enduring and unchanging nature. The Ten Commandments are a concise set of moral and ethical imperatives that guide human conduct and relationships with God and one another. They are typically divided into two sets: the first three commandments focus on the relationship between humans and God, while the remaining seven govern human interactions.

> You shall have no other gods before me. (NIV)
>
> You shall not make for yourself a carved image. (ESV)
>
> You shall not take the name of the Lord your God in vain. (ESV)
>
> Remember the Sabbath day and keep it holy. (NRSV)
>
> Honor your father and mother.
>
> You shall not murder.
>
> You shall not commit adultery.
>
> You shall not steal.
>
> You shall not bear false witness against your neighbor. (NKJV)
>
> You shall not covet.

The Ten Commandments hold profound theological significance within the Catholic faith:

Moral Foundation: They provide a moral foundation for ethical behavior, emphasizing reverence for God and respect for human dignity.

Covenant Relationship: They establish a covenantal relationship between God and humanity, guiding the Israelites in their commitment to God's law.

Universal Relevance: While delivered to the Israelites, the commandments have universal relevance and applicability to all people, transcending cultural and historical boundaries.

Ethical Guidance: They offer ethical guidance for personal conduct, family life, and societal relationships, fostering a just and harmonious community.

Throughout Catholic history, theologians and scholars have elaborated on the Ten Commandments, providing interpretations and applications relevant to various cultural contexts. These interpretations emphasize:

Love of God and Neighbor: Jesus Christ reaffirmed the centrality of the commandments, summarizing them as love for God and love for one's neighbor.

Personal and Social Ethics: The commandments address not only individual morality but also the ethical dimensions of social justice, family life, and community welfare.

Formation of Conscience: They serve as a guide for the formation of conscience, helping individuals discern right from wrong in complex moral situations.

Teaching and Reflection: The Ten Commandments are often used in catechesis, religious education, and moral theology to foster a deeper understanding of Catholic ethics.

Chapter 5: The Historical Books - Chronicles of God's People

The Historical Books of the Old Testament form a compelling narrative tapestry that chronicles the journey of God's chosen people, the Israelites. These books offer a rich and multifaceted account of Israel's history, revealing the complexities of their relationship with God and their interactions with neighboring nations.

The Historical Books encompass a series of texts, including Joshua, Judges, Ruth, 1 Samuel, 2 Samuel, 1 Kings, 2 Kings, 1 Chronicles, 2 Chronicles, Ezra, Nehemiah, and Esther. Together, they provide a detailed narrative of Israel's history, from their entry into the Promised Land to the return from Babylonian exile.

Within the Historical Books, numerous themes and narratives emerge:

Conquest and Settlement: Joshua recounts the Israelites' conquest of Canaan and the division of the land among the twelve tribes.

Leadership and Judges: Judges explores the period of Israelite history characterized by a cycle of sin, oppression, repentance, and deliverance through various judges.

Monarchy and Kings: The books of Samuel, Kings, and Chronicles chronicle the establishment of the Israelite monarchy, the reigns of notable kings such as David and Solomon, and the subsequent division of the kingdom into Israel and Judah.

Prophets and Prophecy: These books feature encounters with prophets who deliver God's messages, offering guidance, warnings, and hope to the people.

Exile and Restoration: The later Historical Books, including Ezra, Nehemiah, and Esther, narrate the exile of the Israelites to Babylon, their eventual return, and the challenges they face in rebuilding their nation.

The Historical Books hold profound theological significance within the Catholic faith:

God's Covenant Faithfulness: The narrative underscores God's enduring faithfulness to His covenant with Israel, even in the face of their faithlessness.

Divine Providence: Throughout the narrative, God's providential care for His people is evident, guiding them through times of victory and defeat.

Human Responsibility: The books reveal the importance of human responsibility and obedience to God's commandments in maintaining the covenant relationship.

Moral and Ethical Lessons: They offer moral and ethical lessons drawn from the experiences of Israel, highlighting the consequences of sin and the rewards of faithfulness.

The Historical Books remain highly relevant in the Catholic faith, offering valuable insights into the complexities of human history, faith, and the divine-human relationship. They prompt reflection on themes of leadership, justice, faithfulness, and the consequences of sin, all of which continue to resonate in the lives of believers today.

Joshua: Entering the Promised Land

The book of Joshua is about the Israelites' long-awaited entry into the Promised Land. Joshua, who succeeded Moses as the leader of the Israelites, plays a central role in this narrative.

Following the death of Moses, Joshua is chosen by God to lead the Israelites into the land of Canaan (Joshua 1:1-9). His name, which means "Yahweh is salvation," encapsulates the theme of God's saving presence throughout the book. One of the most iconic events in the book of Joshua is the miraculous crossing of the Jordan River. Mirroring the parting of the Red Sea during the Exodus, the waters of the Jordan miraculously halt, allowing the Israelites to pass into the Promised Land. Twelve stones are erected as a memorial to this event, emphasizing the importance of remembering God's mighty deeds.

Under Joshua's leadership, the Israelites engage in a series of military campaigns to conquer the land of Canaan, which God promised to their ancestors. These campaigns are guided by divine intervention and strategic military leadership.

- The Battle of Jericho: The city of Jericho is famously conquered through a unique strategy. The Israelites, following God's command, march around the city for seven days, culminating in the walls of Jericho collapsing, leading to its capture.
- Distribution of the Land: After the conquest, the land is divided among the twelve tribes of Israel, in fulfillment of God's promise to Abraham, Isaac, and Jacob.

Throughout the book of Joshua, we see a strong emphasis on covenant renewal. Joshua calls the people to faithfulness and obedience to the Mosaic Law. He famously declares, "As for me and my household, we will serve the Lord" (Joshua 24:15), underscoring the importance of individual and collective commitment to God.

The book of Joshua holds profound theological significance within the Catholic faith:

Fulfillment of God's Promises: It illustrates God's faithfulness in fulfilling His promises, demonstrating that He keeps His word to His people.

Leadership and Obedience: Joshua's leadership serves as a model of obedience, trust, and courage in carrying out God's directives.

Covenant and Commitment: The emphasis on covenant renewal reminds Catholics of their own commitment to follow God's commandments and serve Him faithfully.

Theological Themes: The book explores themes of divine intervention, providence, and the importance of memory in the life of faith.

The story of Joshua entering the Promised Land remains relevant in the Catholic faith as a testament to God's faithfulness and the importance of obedience to His commandments. It inspires believers to reflect on their own journey of faith, the significance of their commitments to God, and the need to trust in His providential guidance. Joshua's legacy of leadership and unwavering faith continues to serve as an enduring example within the Catholic tradition.

Judges: Cycles of Apostasy and Deliverance

The book of Judges is a distinctive and impactful narrative within the Historical Books of the Old Testament. It presents a recurring pattern of human behavior marked by disobedience (apostasy) and deliverance by divinely chosen leaders (judges). The book spans a tumultuous period in Israel's history, following the conquest of Canaan under Joshua's leadership. It covers a time before the Israelites established a centralized monarchy, depicting an era marked by tribal autonomy and sporadic conflicts with neighboring nations.

Central to the narrative are recurring cycles of apostasy and deliverance:

Apostasy: The Israelites turn away from God, often lured by the worship of foreign gods and engaging in sinful practices.

Oppression: As a consequence of their apostasy, God allows foreign oppressors to subjugate the Israelites, subjecting them to hardship and suffering.

Cry for Deliverance: In their distress, the Israelites cry out to God for help, seeking deliverance from their oppressors.

Rise of a Judge: In response to their plea, God raises up a judge—a charismatic and divinely appointed leader—to deliver the people from oppression.

Deliverance: The judge leads the Israelites in military campaigns, achieving victory over their oppressors and securing a period of peace and restoration.

Several judges emerge as key figures in the book of Judges, each demonstrating unique qualities and leadership:

Deborah: A prophetess and judge who played a pivotal role in defeating the Canaanites and inspiring the Israelites to return to God.

Gideon: A humble farmer chosen by God to lead the Israelites against the Midianites, demonstrating God's power through a small army.

Samson: Known for his extraordinary strength and tumultuous personal life, Samson's exploits against the Philistines illustrate God's ability to work through imperfect individuals.

The book of Judges holds profound theological significance within the Catholic faith:

Sin and Consequence: It underscores the consequences of sin and disobedience, revealing that turning away from God leads to suffering and oppression.

Divine Intervention: God's repeated act of raising up judges underscores His mercy and desire to rescue His people, even in their waywardness.

Human Frailty: The judges themselves often exhibit human frailty and imperfection, highlighting the need for divine grace in the face of challenges.

Repentance and Deliverance: The cycle of apostasy and deliverance emphasizes the importance of genuine repentance and the potential for redemption through God's intervention.

The narrative of Judges serves as a poignant reminder within the Catholic faith of the consequences of sin, the need for repentance, and the divine mercy that is readily available to those who turn back to God. It encourages reflection on the role of leadership, the importance of faithfulness, and the enduring cycle of God's forgiveness and deliverance. Judges also remind Catholics of the transformative power of God's grace, even in the midst of human weakness and waywardness.

Kings and Chronicles: Israel's Monarchy

The books of Kings and Chronicles provide an in-depth historical account of Israel's transition from tribal leadership to monarchy. These books chronicle the reigns of Israel's kings, their successes, failures, and the profound spiritual and political developments that shaped the nation. The book of Kings begins with the establishment of Israel's monarchy under the leadership of King Saul. It covers the reigns of successive kings, primarily focusing on the Northern Kingdom of Israel and the Southern Kingdom of Judah. Key events and rulers include:

Saul: The first king of Israel, chosen by God, but whose disobedience led to his downfall.

David: Renowned as Israel's greatest king, David's reign is marked by military victories, the establishment of Jerusalem as the capital, and his covenant with God.

Solomon: David's son, known for his wisdom, the construction of the Temple in Jerusalem, and his gradual drift away from God.

The Divided Kingdom: Following Solomon's reign, the kingdom is divided into Israel (the Northern Kingdom) and Judah (the Southern Kingdom), each with its own line of kings.

Prophets and Their Messages: Prophets like Elijah and Elisha play a crucial role in challenging unfaithful kings and calling the people back to God.

The Fall of Israel: Israel falls to the Assyrians in 722 BCE due to its idolatry and disobedience to God.

The Exile of Judah: Judah eventually falls to the Babylonians in 586 BCE, leading to the exile of its people.

The books of Chronicles provide a parallel account of Israel's history, with a particular emphasis on the religious aspects of the monarchy. This includes the construction of the Temple in Jerusalem by Solomon, the liturgical practices, and the genealogies of key figures.

The books of Kings and Chronicles hold profound theological significance within the Catholic faith:

Leadership and Accountability: They highlight the importance of leadership and the moral accountability of kings before God and His law.

Divine Covenant and Temple: The construction of the Temple symbolizes God's dwelling among His people and the covenantal relationship between God and Israel.

Prophetic Witness: The prophetic voices in these books serve as instruments of God's call to faithfulness and moral responsibility.

The Consequences of Sin: The downfall of the Northern Kingdom and the exile of Judah underscore the consequences of sin and disobedience.

The books of Kings and Chronicles remain highly relevant in the Catholic faith:

- Moral Leadership: They offer lessons on the qualities of moral leadership and the consequences of unfaithfulness.
- Covenant and Worship: They underscore the significance of the covenant relationship with God and the centrality of worship in the life of God's people.
- Prophetic Tradition: They emphasize the prophetic tradition's role in challenging injustice and unfaithfulness in society.
- Reflection on History: They prompt Catholics to reflect on the lessons of history and the enduring call to remain faithful to God's commandments.

By exploring these texts, believers gain insight into the challenges and complexities of leadership, the importance of religious fidelity, and the enduring consequences of moral choices. They also inspire Catholics to deepen their commitment to God's covenant and engage in worship as a means of drawing closer to the Divine.

Chapter 6: The Wisdom Books - Insights for Life

In the pages of the Old Testament, there exists a treasure trove of wisdom that transcends time and circumstance. This wisdom is found within the poetic and philosophical works known as the Wisdom Books. These texts offer profound insights into the human experience, the pursuit of virtue, the nature of God, and the quest for meaning and understanding in a complex world.

The Wisdom Books include several captivating texts, each contributing unique perspectives on the human condition and divine wisdom:

Job: A profound exploration of suffering, faith, and the mystery of God's providence.

Psalms: A collection of poetic prayers and songs that express a wide range of human emotions, from joy and praise to lament and sorrow.

Proverbs: A compilation of practical wisdom, offering guidance on ethical living, virtues, and the pursuit of knowledge.

Ecclesiastes: A philosophical reflection on the meaning of life, the pursuit of happiness, and the inevitability of death.

Song of Solomon: An allegorical poem celebrating love, often interpreted as a reflection of the divine love between God and His people.

Wisdom of Solomon: A work that explores the pursuit of wisdom and its connection to God's plan for humanity.

Sirach (Ecclesiasticus): A collection of ethical teachings and practical advice for virtuous living.

The Wisdom Books offer a rich tapestry of themes and teachings:

- The Nature of Wisdom: They delve into the nature of wisdom itself, portraying it as a cherished and transformative virtue.
- Human Suffering and Divine Justice: Job and other texts grapple with the profound questions of human suffering and the justice of God.
- Prayer and Praise: The Psalms provide a diverse range of prayers and hymns, serving as a guide for worship and personal devotion.
- Virtue and Ethics: Proverbs, Sirach, and other texts offer practical advice on living virtuously and making ethical choices.
- Existential Reflection: Ecclesiastes contemplates the meaning of life, the pursuit of happiness, and the inevitability of death.
- Love and Allegory: The Song of Solomon explores the themes of love and longing, often seen as an allegory for the divine-human relationship.

The Wisdom Books hold profound theological significance within the Catholic faith:

- The Search for Wisdom: They emphasize the search for wisdom as a noble and transformative pursuit.
- Prayer and Worship: The Psalms continue to serve as a source of inspiration for prayer and worship within the Catholic tradition.
- Moral and Ethical Guidance: Proverbs and Sirach offer practical guidance for ethical living.
- Suffering and Redemption: Job wrestles with the profound questions of suffering and the ultimate mystery of redemption.
- Existential Reflection: Ecclesiastes prompts believers to contemplate the deeper questions of existence and the quest for meaning.

The Wisdom Books remain profoundly relevant in the Catholic faith, offering timeless wisdom for navigating the complexities of life. They inspire believers to deepen their relationship with God, cultivate virtues, seek understanding, and find solace in times of trial.

Proverbs: Practical Wisdom

Among the Wisdom Books of the Old Testament, the book of Proverbs stands out as a collection of practical and timeless wisdom. Its pages are filled with aphorisms, sayings, and guidance that provide essential principles for ethical living, virtuous behavior, and the pursuit of wisdom. The book of Proverbs is a compilation of concise and memorable sayings that offer insights into various aspects of life. These proverbs are often framed as fatherly advice to a son, emphasizing the importance of acquiring wisdom, understanding, and virtue. The book is traditionally attributed to King Solomon, renowned for his wisdom, but it also includes contributions from other wise individuals.

Proverbs covers a wide range of themes and teachings, making it a valuable guide for ethical living:

- The Pursuit of Wisdom: The central theme of Proverbs is the pursuit of wisdom, which is portrayed as more precious than gold or silver. It encourages readers to seek understanding and discernment.
- Virtuous Living: The book provides practical guidance on living virtuously, cultivating qualities such as honesty, humility, diligence, and kindness.
- The Consequences of Actions: Proverbs frequently highlights the consequences of one's actions, whether positive or negative. It emphasizes the principle of sowing and reaping.
- Speech and Communication: The book offers insights into the power of words and communication, cautioning against gossip, lying, and quarreling.

- Parental Guidance: Many proverbs are presented as advice from a father to his son, emphasizing the importance of parental instruction and moral guidance.
- The Fear of the Lord: Proverbs teaches that the fear of the Lord is the beginning of wisdom. It underscores the significance of a reverent and obedient relationship with God.

Proverbs is filled with practical guidance for daily life:

- Work Ethic: It encourages diligence in one's work and warns against laziness.
- Financial Responsibility: The book provides financial wisdom, advocating for prudence and avoiding debt.
- Friendships and Relationships: Proverbs offers insights into building healthy relationships and avoiding the pitfalls of association with the wicked.
- Humility and Teachability: It underscores the value of humility, teachability, and the willingness to accept correction.
- Forgiveness and Reconciliation: Proverbs encourages forgiveness and reconciliation in relationships.

The book of Proverbs holds profound theological significance within the Catholic faith:

- Virtue and Holiness: It emphasizes the importance of living virtuously and pursuing holiness in daily life.
- Divine Guidance: The pursuit of wisdom is seen as a path to God's guidance and favor.
- Responsibility and Accountability: Proverbs underscores the individual's responsibility for their choices and actions, leading to accountability before God.
- Humility and Obedience: It promotes humility before God and obedience to His commands.

Proverbs remains highly relevant in the Catholic faith, offering practical and moral guidance for believers seeking to live virtuous lives. Its timeless wisdom transcends cultural and historical boundaries, providing valuable insights for individuals and communities. Catholics turn to Proverbs as a source of ethical principles, guidance for decision-making, and a reminder of the enduring pursuit of wisdom as a lifelong journey.

Job: Wrestling with Suffering

The book of Job is a profound and enigmatic work within the Wisdom Books of the Old Testament. It grapples with one of the most profound and enduring questions of human existence: the nature of suffering and the response of faith in the face of adversity. The book tells the story of a man named Job, described as blameless and upright, who experiences a series of devastating losses and unimaginable suffering. Job's life unravels as he loses his wealth, health, and even his family. Despite his afflictions, Job maintains his faithfulness to God, even as he grapples with profound questions about the nature of suffering and the justice of God.

The book of Job explores deep and complex themes:

- Suffering and Innocence: It raises questions about the suffering of the innocent and the apparent absence of justice in the world.
- Theodicy: Job's lamentations and dialogues with his friends delve into theodicy, the question of why a just and loving God permits suffering.
- Human Limitations: Job confronts the limitations of human understanding and the mystery of God's ways.
- Faith and Trust: Despite his suffering, Job maintains his faith in God, even as he questions God's actions.
- Divine Response: In the latter part of the book, God responds to Job, challenging him to contemplate the intricacies of creation and divine wisdom.
- Repentance and Restoration: Ultimately, Job repents of his complaints and is restored to prosperity, emphasizing the importance of trust and humility before God.

The book of Job remains profoundly relevant in the Catholic faith:

- Theodicy and Faith: It challenges believers to wrestle with the question of suffering and to deepen their faith in God's providence.
- Compassion and Empathy: It encourages compassion and empathy for those who are suffering, acknowledging the deep emotional and spiritual struggles they may face.
- Trust in God: Job's trust in God, even amid adversity, inspires Catholics to maintain their faith in times of trial.
- The Mystery of God: It prompts reflection on the unfathomable mystery of God's ways and the need for humility in our understanding.

Job's story serves as a profound meditation on the human condition and the complexities of faith in the face of suffering. It invites believers to engage in a deep and reflective dialogue with God, acknowledging that even in the midst of life's most profound challenges, faith can endure, and God's presence can be found.

Ecclesiastes: The Meaning of Life

The book of Ecclesiastes, also known as Qoheleth, is a philosophical and reflective work within the Wisdom Books of the Old Testament. It grapples with the fundamental questions of human existence, the pursuit of happiness, and the enigma of life's meaning. Ecclesiastes is written in the voice of Qoheleth, often translated as "the Teacher" or "the Preacher." Qoheleth is a seeker of wisdom and truth, and his reflections take the form of philosophical musings and observations on life's complexities.

The book of Ecclesiastes delves into a range of existential themes:

- The Pursuit of Happiness: Qoheleth embarks on a quest to find happiness and meaning in various pursuits, including wisdom, pleasure, work, and wealth.

- The Vanity of Life: Qoheleth repeatedly uses the term "vanity" (or "meaningless") to describe the fleeting and ephemeral nature of human endeavors. He observes that all human achievements are transitory.

- The Inevitability of Death: The reality of mortality is a central theme. Qoheleth contemplates the certainty of death and its impact on the meaning of life.

- God's Sovereignty: Qoheleth acknowledges the sovereignty of God and the limitations of human understanding in comprehending divine purposes.

- Enjoyment of Life: Amid his reflections on life's challenges, Qoheleth encourages readers to find joy and contentment in the present moment and to appreciate life's simple pleasures.

The book of Ecclesiastes holds profound theological significance within the Catholic faith:

- Human Limitation: It underscores the limitations of human knowledge and the mysteries of God's providence.

- The Quest for Meaning: Qoheleth's search for meaning prompts Catholics to reflect on the purpose of life and the pursuit of lasting happiness.

- Divine Perspective: The book encourages believers to acknowledge God's sovereignty and trust in His divine plan, even when life appears enigmatic.

- Living Mindfully: Ecclesiastes challenges individuals to live mindfully, recognizing the value of the present moment and the blessings of life.

Ecclesiastes remains profoundly relevant in the Catholic faith:

- The Pursuit of Meaning: It prompts Catholics to engage in a thoughtful exploration of life's purpose and the pursuit of authentic happiness.

- Humility and Trust: Qoheleth's reflections foster humility before the mysteries of God and trust in His providence.

- Appreciation of Life: The book encourages a deep appreciation of life's transient beauty and the importance of gratitude for God's gifts.

- A Call to Reflect: Ecclesiastes invites Catholics to reflect on the brevity of life and the significance of living in accordance with God's will.

In the midst of life's uncertainties and existential questions, Ecclesiastes invites believers to embrace the enigma of existence with trust in God's sovereignty and to find meaning in the simplicity of life, recognizing that true fulfillment is ultimately found in a relationship with the Divine.

Chapter 7: The Prophets - God's Messengers

In the tapestry of the Old Testament, the prophetic books stand as a unique and vibrant thread, weaving together the messages of God's chosen messengers to His people. These prophets were called to deliver divine words of warning, encouragement, and hope, often in times of great historical and spiritual significance. The prophetic tradition in the Old Testament is a rich tapestry of diverse voices and messages. Prophets served as God's intermediaries, conveying His will to His people. Their messages encompassed various themes, including calls to repentance, social justice, divine promises, and glimpses into the future.

The prophetic books are often categorized into major and minor prophets, not based on their significance but on the length of their writings. The major prophets include figures like Isaiah, Jeremiah, and Ezekiel, who authored longer books. The minor prophets, on the other hand, contributed shorter works, including Hosea, Joel, Amos, and others.

The prophetic books explore a wide range of themes and teachings:

- Call to Repentance: Prophets frequently called the people to turn away from sin and return to God in repentance.
- Social Justice: They championed social justice, denouncing oppression, exploitation, and the mistreatment of the vulnerable.
- Divine Promises: Prophets conveyed God's promises of restoration, renewal, and the coming of the Messiah.
- Warnings and Consequences: They warned of the consequences of disobedience and the potential for divine judgment.
- Messianic Prophecies: Prophets foretold the coming of a Messiah who would bring salvation and usher in a new covenant.

The prophetic books hold profound theological significance within the Catholic faith:

- God's Faithfulness: They reveal God's faithfulness to His covenant and His enduring love for His people.
- The Call to Holiness: Prophets challenge believers to pursue holiness, righteousness, and justice in their lives.
- Hope and Redemption: They offer messages of hope and redemption, even in the face of suffering and exile.
- Messianic Fulfillment: Many prophecies find their fulfillment in the life, death, and resurrection of Jesus Christ.

The prophetic books continue to be profoundly relevant in the Catholic faith:

- Moral Guidance: They provide moral and ethical guidance, challenging believers to live according to God's commandments.
- Social Justice: Prophetic calls for justice inspire Catholics to advocate for the marginalized and work for a more just society.
- Hope and Redemption: The messages of hope and redemption offer solace and assurance in times of trial.
- Messianic Hope: They point to the fulfillment of Messianic prophecies in the person of Jesus Christ, reinforcing the central message of the Gospel.

As we explore the prophetic books, we encounter the enduring relevance of their messages, their call to repentance and holiness, and their profound insights into God's plan for humanity. The prophets serve as a bridge between the Old and New Testaments, connecting the promises of old with the fulfillment found in Christ, making their messages vital for all seekers of faith.

Isaiah: The Suffering Servant

The book of Isaiah, one of the major prophetic works in the Old Testament, is a rich and complex text that addresses themes of prophecy, redemption, and the coming Messiah. Within the book of Isaiah, a particularly poignant and central figure emerges—the

Suffering Servant. Isaiah, the prophet, lived during the 8th century BCE and was called by God to deliver messages of both judgment and hope to the people of Judah and Jerusalem. His prophetic ministry spanned several decades and encompassed the tumultuous times of the Assyrian threat and the eventual exile of Judah.

Isaiah contains four distinct passages known as the Suffering Servant Songs (Isaiah 42:1-4, 49:1-6, 50:4-9, and 52:13-53:12). These songs describe a mysterious figure—the Suffering Servant—who is called to fulfill a unique and sacrificial role in God's plan of redemption. The songs poignantly depict this Servant's suffering, rejection, and ultimate vindication.

The Suffering Servant Songs within Isaiah convey profound themes and teachings:

- Sacrificial Redemption: The Suffering Servant willingly offers Himself as a sacrifice for the sins of others, bearing their iniquities.
- Identification with Humanity: He identifies with the suffering and sin of humanity, experiencing rejection, affliction, and even death.
- Divine Restoration: The Servant's suffering leads to divine restoration and the forgiveness of sins for those who believe.
- Vindication and Exaltation: Despite His suffering and rejection, the Servant is ultimately vindicated and exalted by God.
- Universal Salvation: The scope of the Servant's mission extends to all nations, bringing salvation to the ends of the earth.

Isaiah's Suffering Servant holds profound theological significance within the Catholic faith:

- Messiah and Redemption: The Servant Songs foreshadow the mission of the Messiah, Jesus Christ, as the ultimate Suffering Servant who redeems humanity through His sacrificial death.

- Redemption and Forgiveness: They emphasize the redemptive power of suffering and the forgiveness of sins through the atoning work of Christ.
- Identification with Christ: Isaiah's prophecy strengthens the identification of Jesus Christ as the fulfillment of Old Testament prophecies.
- Universal Salvation: The Servant's mission highlights God's plan for universal salvation, extending the offer of redemption to all.

Isaiah's Suffering Servant Songs continue to resonate with Catholics, serving as a powerful reminder of the depth of God's love and the transformative nature of Christ's redemptive mission. They invite believers to embrace the message of forgiveness, restoration, and hope found in the ultimate Suffering Servant, Jesus Christ.

Jeremiah: The Weeping Prophet

The book of Jeremiah, situated within the prophetic literature of the Old Testament, introduces us to the life and ministry of a unique prophet—Jeremiah, often referred to as the "Weeping Prophet." Jeremiah's prophetic journey is marked by a deep sense of sorrow and lament as he delivers God's messages of judgment and impending exile to rebellious people. Jeremiah's prophetic calling, as recorded in Jeremiah 1:4-10, reveals God's selection of him as a prophet to the nations. Despite his initial reluctance, Jeremiah accepts the divine commission to speak God's words to Israel and the nations, even as he anticipates the challenges and suffering that will accompany his mission.

Jeremiah's prophetic ministry covers a range of themes:

- National Apostasy: Jeremiah addresses the rampant idolatry and apostasy in Israel and Judah, emphasizing the need for repentance and faithfulness to God's covenant.
- Divine Judgment: He announces God's judgment upon the nations, including Israel and Judah, for their disobedience and idolatry.

- Suffering and Lament: Jeremiah's personal suffering and lamentations are interwoven with his prophetic messages, reflecting his deep empathy for the people and the pain of their impending exile.
- The New Covenant: Jeremiah prophesies the coming of a new covenant, where God's law will be written on the hearts of His people, emphasizing a personal and transformative relationship with God.

Jeremiah's prophetic ministry holds profound theological significance within the Catholic faith:

- Faithful Obedience: Jeremiah's unwavering faithfulness to God's call, despite the suffering it entailed, serves as a model of obedient service.
- Repentance and Forgiveness: His call to repentance and God's offer of forgiveness demonstrate God's desire for reconciliation and mercy.
- The New Covenant: Jeremiah's prophecy of the new covenant anticipates the transformative work of Jesus Christ, who fulfills this promise in the New Testament.
- Lament and Empathy: Jeremiah's expressions of lament and empathy remind Catholics of the importance of compassion and intercessory prayer for those who are suffering.

Jeremiah's prophetic ministry is a poignant reminder of the prophet's role as a faithful messenger of God's word, even in the face of opposition and personal suffering. His life and message continue to resonate with believers, inviting them to embrace faithful obedience, hope in God's mercy, and a compassionate heart for those in need.

Ezekiel: Visions and Prophecies

The book of Ezekiel, nestled within the prophetic writings of the Old Testament, introduces us to the enigmatic prophet Ezekiel. His ministry was marked by vivid visions, symbolic actions, and profound prophecies, all delivered during a time of exile.

In this subchapter, "Ezekiel: Visions and Prophecies," we explore the significance of Ezekiel's prophetic ministry within the Catholic faith and the profound insights it offers into God's presence and providence.

Ezekiel: The Visionary Prophet

Ezekiel, a priest and prophet, was among the exiles taken from Jerusalem to Babylon in 597 BCE. His prophetic call came in a dramatic vision of God's glory—a vision often referred to as the "chariot throne" vision (Ezekiel 1). This initial encounter with God set the tone for Ezekiel's prophetic ministry and the extraordinary visions and messages he would receive.

Ezekiel's prophetic ministry covers a wide range of themes:

- Divine Presence: Ezekiel's visions emphasize God's presence among His people, even in the midst of exile.
- Sin and Judgment: He delivers messages of judgment against the sins of Israel and the surrounding nations, highlighting the consequences of disobedience.
- Hope and Restoration: Alongside messages of judgment, Ezekiel also prophesies hope and restoration, including the vision of the dry bones (Ezekiel 37), symbolizing the restoration of Israel.
- Shepherd Imagery: Ezekiel employs shepherd imagery to describe God as the caring and just shepherd who seeks His scattered sheep.
- The New Temple: He envisions a future temple where God's glory will dwell, foreshadowing the spiritual temple in the New Testament.

Ezekiel's prophetic ministry, characterized by visions, prophecies, and symbolic actions, reminds Catholics of God's unwavering presence, His call to repentance, and His promise of restoration. It encourages believers to trust in God's providence and to seek His guidance and care, even in the midst of life's complexities.

Chapter 8: Psalms and the Poetry of Worship

In the rich tapestry of the Old Testament, there is a treasure trove of sacred poetry that has captivated the hearts of believers for millennia. Among these poetic expressions, the Psalms stand out as a collection of songs and prayers that have been sung, recited, and meditated upon by countless generations of faithful. The book of Psalms, also known as the Psalter, is a collection of 150 individual psalms, traditionally attributed to King David and other psalmists. These psalms encompass a wide range of emotions and themes, from praise and thanksgiving to lament and supplication. They have been described as the "prayer book of the Bible" and are a central component of the liturgical life of the Church.

The Psalms cover a vast array of themes and teachings:

- Worship and Praise: Many psalms exalt God's greatness, His creation, and His wondrous deeds, inviting believers to join in the chorus of praise.
- Lament and Suffering: Other psalms express deep sorrow, lamenting personal or communal suffering and crying out to God for help and deliverance.
- Confidence and Trust: Certain psalms convey unwavering confidence in God's protection, providence, and faithfulness.
- Penitence and Forgiveness: Some psalms acknowledge human sinfulness and the need for repentance, seeking God's forgiveness and mercy.
- Messianic Prophecy: Several psalms contain Messianic prophecies, pointing forward to the coming of a Savior, such as Psalm 22, a vivid foreshadowing of Christ's crucifixion.

The Psalms hold profound theological significance within the Catholic faith:

- Emotional Expression: The psalms teach that it is acceptable to bring all emotions, including doubt, anger, and despair, into one's relationship with God.

- Spiritual Sustenance: They provide spiritual nourishment, offering comfort, guidance, and inspiration to Catholics in their daily lives.
- Christological Insights: The Messianic psalms offer insights into the identity and mission of Jesus Christ, deepening the understanding of His role as Savior.

Relevance in the Catholic Faith

The Psalms continue to be profoundly relevant in the Catholic faith:

- Liturgy and Prayer: They are integral to the liturgical life of the Church and serve as a wellspring of personal and communal prayer.
- Comfort and Consolation: The psalms offer comfort and consolation to Catholics facing trials and tribulations.
- Personal Devotion: Believers can turn to the Psalms for guidance and inspiration in their personal spiritual journeys.
- Messianic Fulfillment: The Messianic psalms affirm the fulfillment of Old Testament prophecies in the life, death, and resurrection of Jesus Christ.

As we delve into the Psalms, we discover a profound well of spirituality, offering words of praise, solace in suffering, and a glimpse into the human-divine encounter. The Psalms remain a timeless source of comfort and inspiration for all who seek to draw closer to God through the poetry of worship.

The Book of Psalms: Prayers and Praises

The book of Psalms, nestled in the heart of the Old Testament, is a poetic and spiritual treasure trove that has profoundly impacted the worship and devotion of Catholics and believers of various faith traditions for centuries. Comprising 150 individual psalms, this collection of sacred poetry serves as a testament to the rich tapestry of human emotions and experiences, all brought before the Divine in the form of prayers, praises, and meditations.

The Psalms are categorized into various genres and themes, each offering a unique perspective on the human-divine relationship:

- Psalms of Praise and Thanksgiving: These psalms extol the greatness of God, His creation, and His mighty deeds. Psalm 100, known as the "Jubilate Deo," is a classic example of a psalm of praise.

- Psalms of Lament: These psalms express deep sorrow, grief, or distress. They cry out to God in times of personal or communal suffering, seeking His intervention. Psalm 22, "My God, my God, why have you forsaken me? (NIV)" is a well-known lament.

- Psalms of Confidence and Trust: These psalms proclaim unwavering confidence in God's protection, guidance, and faithfulness. Psalm 23, "The Lord is my shepherd," is a beloved example of trust in God's care.

- Psalms of Penitence and Forgiveness: These psalms acknowledge human sinfulness and the need for repentance. They seek God's forgiveness and mercy. Psalm 51, a penitential psalm, is attributed to King David.

- Psalms of Wisdom: These psalms offer moral and ethical guidance, emphasizing the importance of living a righteous life. Psalm 1 is a notable example of a wisdom psalm.

- Messianic Psalms: Several psalms contain Messianic prophecies, foretelling the coming of a Savior. Psalm 110, for instance, speaks of the Messiah's eternal priesthood.

The Psalms hold profound theological significance within the Catholic faith:

- Prayer and Worship: They provide a model for authentic and heartfelt prayer and worship, inviting believers to engage deeply with God.

- Emotional Expression: The psalms demonstrate that it is acceptable to bring the full range of human emotions and experiences into one's relationship with God.

- Spiritual Sustenance: They offer spiritual nourishment, providing comfort, guidance, and inspiration for Catholics in their daily lives.

- Messianic Fulfillment: The Messianic psalms affirm the fulfillment of Old Testament prophecies in the person of Jesus Christ, deepening the understanding of His role as Savior.

The Psalms continue to be profoundly relevant in the Catholic faith:

- Liturgy and Prayer: They play an integral role in the liturgical life of the Church, enriching the Mass and the Liturgy of the Hours.
- Comfort and Consolation: The psalms offer comfort and consolation to Catholics facing trials and tribulations, reminding them of God's presence.
- Personal Devotion: Believers turn to the Psalms for personal meditation and devotion, finding solace and inspiration in their words.
- Christological Insights: The Messianic psalms deepen the understanding of Jesus Christ as the fulfillment of Old Testament prophecies, reinforcing His central role in the Catholic faith.

The Book of Psalms, with its poetic beauty and spiritual depth, continues to be a source of solace, inspiration, and devotion for Catholics. It invites believers to engage in a profound and intimate dialogue with God, bringing their joys, sorrows, and praises before the Divine, and finding spiritual nourishment in the poetry of worship.

Types of Psalms and Their Uses

The book of Psalms is a diverse collection of sacred poetry, encompassing a wide range of emotions and themes. These psalms have been used in worship, meditation, and personal devotion for centuries, serving as a wellspring of spiritual nourishment for Catholics and believers of various faith traditions. To fully appreciate the Psalms, it's essential to understand the various types of psalms and their distinct uses within the context of the Catholic faith.

1. Psalms of Praise and Thanksgiving

These psalms extol the greatness of God, His marvelous works, and His creative power. They are songs of adoration and gratitude, inviting worshippers to join in the chorus of praise. Psalms of praise and thanksgiving are commonly used in liturgical settings to celebrate God's majesty and providence. They remind believers of the importance of recognizing God's blessings and expressing gratitude.

Example: Psalm 100 - "Make a joyful noise to the Lord, all the earth! Serve the Lord with gladness! Come into his presence with singing! (ESV)"

2. Psalms of Lament

Lament psalms give voice to deep sorrow, grief, or distress. They are expressions of anguish and a cry for God's intervention in times of personal or communal suffering. Lament psalms encourage believers to be honest about their pain and to seek solace in God's presence. These psalms are particularly relevant during times of trial and hardship, reminding Catholics that it is acceptable to bring their pain before God.

Example: Psalm 22 - "My God, my God, why have you forsaken me? Why are you so far from saving me, from the words of my groaning? (ESV)"

3. Psalms of Confidence and Trust

These psalms declare unwavering confidence in God's protection, guidance, and faithfulness. They express trust in God's care and provision, even in the face of adversity. Psalms of confidence and trust offer assurance to believers that God is their refuge and strength. They encourage Catholics to rely on God's unfailing love and to seek His guidance in their daily lives.

Example: Psalm 23 - "The Lord is my shepherd; I shall not want. He makes me lie down in green pastures. He leads me beside still waters. (ESV)"

4. Psalms of Penitence and Forgiveness

Penitential psalms acknowledge human sinfulness and the need for repentance. They are prayers of contrition and a plea for God's mercy and forgiveness. These psalms remind Catholics of the importance of humility and the Sacrament of Reconciliation. They encourage believers to turn to God with contrite hearts and seek His pardoning grace.

Example: Psalm 51 - "Create in me a clean heart, O God, and renew a right spirit within me. Cast me not away from your presence, and take not your Holy Spirit from me. (ESV)"

5. Psalms of Wisdom

Wisdom psalms offer moral and ethical guidance, emphasizing the importance of living a righteous life. They provide insights into the blessings of following God's commandments and the consequences of wickedness. These psalms encourage Catholics to seek wisdom and understanding in their daily choices and actions.

Example: Psalm 1 - "Blessed is the man who walks not in the counsel of the wicked, nor stands in the way of sinners, nor sits in the seat of scoffers. (ESV)"

6. Messianic Psalms

Messianic psalms contain prophecies and foreshadowings of the coming Messiah, Jesus Christ. They offer glimpses into the identity and mission of the Savior. Messianic psalms deepen the understanding of Christ's role as the fulfillment of Old Testament prophecies and His central significance in the Catholic faith.

Example: Psalm 110 - "The Lord says to my Lord: 'Sit at my right hand, until I make your enemies your footstool. (ESV)'"

Chapter 9: The Messianic Hope - Foreshadowing Christ

Throughout the Old Testament, a profound and prophetic message echoes—a message of hope, redemption, and the promise of a Savior. This message, known as the Messianic hope, is interwoven into the very fabric of the Old Testament, foreshadowing the arrival of Jesus Christ, the long-awaited Messiah.

From the earliest pages of the Old Testament, the Messianic hope begins to take shape. The promise of a future Deliverer, an Anointed One (Messiah), who will bring salvation and establish God's kingdom, reverberates throughout the sacred text. This hope is like a thread that weaves its way through the stories, prophecies, and symbols of the Old Testament, ultimately finding fulfillment in Jesus Christ.

The Old Testament contains a plethora of Messianic prophecies—foretellings of the coming Messiah's identity, mission, and attributes. These prophecies provide a blueprint for recognizing Jesus Christ as the fulfillment of God's promise to humanity.

Beyond explicit prophecies, the Old Testament employs symbols, types, and foreshadowings that point to Christ. These include figures like Joseph, David, and Jonah, who prefigure aspects of the Messiah's life and mission. Understanding the Messianic hope within the Old Testament holds profound theological significance within the Catholic faith:

- Fulfillment in Christ: It underscores Jesus Christ as the fulfillment of Old Testament promises, reinforcing His role as the Savior and Redeemer.
- God's Faithfulness: The Messianic hope demonstrates God's faithfulness to His covenant and His unwavering commitment to humanity's salvation.
- Unity of Scripture: It highlights the unity of the Old and New Testaments, emphasizing the continuity of God's plan of salvation.

- Hope and Redemption: The Messianic hope inspires hope and offers a profound sense of redemption to Catholics, assuring them of God's providential care.

The Messianic hope remains profoundly relevant in the Catholic faith:

- Christological Understanding: It deepens the understanding of Jesus Christ as the Messiah and reinforces His central role in the faith.
- Salvation and Redemption: The Messianic hope assures Catholics of the possibility of salvation and redemption through faith in Christ.
- Scriptural Connection: It fosters a deeper connection with the Old Testament and enhances Catholics' appreciation of the Old Testament's role in the faith.
- Hope and Encouragement: The Messianic hope offers hope and encouragement to Catholics, reminding them of God's promise of salvation in Christ.

Prophecies of the Messiah

The Old Testament contains a remarkable tapestry of prophecies that anticipate the coming of the Messiah, the promised Savior of humanity. These prophetic passages, spread throughout various books of the Old Testament, offer glimpses into the Messiah's identity, mission, and significance.

Isaiah: The Prophet of the Messiah

The book of Isaiah, often referred to as the "Fifth Gospel," is a treasure trove of Messianic prophecies. Isaiah's prophecies, written during a time of national crisis, offer hope and reassurance through promises of a future Deliverer. Several notable Messianic passages from Isaiah include:

- Isaiah 7:14: The prophecy of the virgin birth - "Therefore the Lord himself will give you a sign. Behold, the virgin shall conceive and bear a son, and shall call his name Immanuel. (ESV)"

- Isaiah 9:6: The prophecy of the Child to be born - "For to us a child is born, to us a son is given; and the government shall be upon his shoulder, and his name shall be called Wonderful Counselor, Mighty God, Everlasting Father, Prince of Peace. (ESV)"
- Isaiah 53: The prophecy of the Suffering Servant - This chapter vividly describes the suffering and atonement of the Messiah, foretelling His redemptive work.

Micah: The Bethlehem Prophecy

The book of Micah contains a well-known prophecy about the birthplace of the Messiah:

- Micah 5:2: "But you, O Bethlehem Ephrathah, who are too little to be among the clans of Judah, from you shall come forth for me one who is to be ruler in Israel, whose coming forth is from of old, from ancient days. (ESV)"

This prophecy foretells that the Messiah will be born in Bethlehem, a fulfillment witnessed in the New Testament with the birth of Jesus in Bethlehem.

Psalms: Messianic Psalms

The Psalms, in addition to their diverse themes, contain Messianic prophecies and foreshadowings. These psalms provide insight into the Messiah's suffering, kingship, and ultimate triumph:

- Psalm 22: A vivid portrayal of the Messiah's suffering and crucifixion, with the famous words, "My God, my God, why have you forsaken me?"
- Psalm 110: Declares the Messiah's eternal priesthood and lordship, with the proclamation, "The Lord says to my Lord: 'Sit at my right hand until I make your enemies your footstool.'"

Zechariah: The Prophecy of the Humble King

The book of Zechariah offers a unique perspective on the Messiah's character:

- Zechariah 9:9: "Rejoice greatly, O daughter of Zion! Shout, Daughter of Jerusalem! See, your king comes to you, righteous and victorious, lowly and riding on a donkey, on a colt, the foal of a donkey. (NIV)"

This prophecy foretells the Messiah's humble entry into Jerusalem, an event commemorated on Palm Sunday in the Christian liturgical calendar.

The prophecies of the Messiah in the Old Testament are like signposts along the road of salvation history, guiding believers to the fulfillment of God's promises in Jesus Christ. They invite Catholics to delve deeper into the scriptural tapestry of the Old Testament, recognizing the Messiah's role as the Redeemer and Savior of all.

Mary and the Old Testament

In the Catholic faith, the connection between Mary, the Mother of Jesus, and the Old Testament is a profound and spiritually enriching aspect of Marian theology. While the Old Testament primarily foreshadows the coming of the Messiah, it also provides a backdrop for understanding Mary's unique role in God's plan of salvation.

1. The Protoevangelium in Genesis

The first allusion to Mary in the Old Testament can be found in the Protoevangelium, also known as the "First Gospel." This passage is found in Genesis 3:15, where God addresses the serpent following the Fall of Adam and Eve:

- "I will put enmity between you and the woman, and between your offspring and hers; he will crush your head, and you will strike his heel. (NIV)"

This verse is traditionally interpreted as the promise of a future Redeemer who will be born of a woman and conquer sin and evil. In Catholic theology, Mary is seen as the "woman" in this prophecy, and Jesus, her Son, fulfills the role of the promised Redeemer.

2. Mary as the New Eve

The parallel between Mary and Eve, the first woman in the Old Testament, is a significant theme in Catholic Marian theology. While Eve's disobedience in the Garden of Eden led to humanity's fall into sin, Mary's obedience and "yes" to God's plan in the Annunciation represent a pivotal moment of redemption. Mary is often referred to as the "New Eve" because her cooperation with God's will leads to the birth of Jesus, who offers salvation to humanity.

3. The Annunciation and Mary's Fiat

The Annunciation, as described in the New Testament's Gospel of Luke (Luke 1:26-38), is a moment that bridges the Old and New Testaments. Mary's response to the angel Gabriel's message, "Let it be done to me according to your word" (Luke 1:38), echoes the obedience of faithful figures in the Old Testament, such as Abraham and Moses. Mary's fiat (Latin for "let it be done") signifies her complete surrender to God's plan and her role as the Mother of the Savior.

4. Mary as the New Covenant's Ark

The Old Testament contains descriptions of the Ark of the Covenant, a sacred container that held the tablets of the Ten Commandments, the manna from heaven, and Aaron's rod. In the New Testament, Mary is seen as the Ark of the New Covenant because, just as the Ark held the Word of God (the Commandments), the Bread of Life (manna), and the authority of the priesthood (Aaron's rod), Mary bore Jesus Christ, who is the living Word of God, the Bread of Life, and the eternal High Priest.

5. Mary's Presence at Key Moments

Throughout the Gospels, Mary is present at significant events in Jesus' life, mirroring the role of the Ark of the Covenant in the Old Testament, which accompanied the Israelites on their journey. Mary is present at the Nativity, the Wedding at Cana, the Crucifixion, and the Pentecost, emphasizing her connection to the pivotal moments of salvation history.

Mary's connection to the Old Testament enriches the Catholic faith in several ways:

- Marian Devotion: It deepens Marian devotion and underscores Mary's role as the Mother of God.
- Theological Understanding: It enhances theological understanding by highlighting Mary's pivotal place in salvation history.
- Liturgical Significance: Mary's presence is celebrated in the liturgical calendar through feasts and solemnities, emphasizing her importance in the life of the Church.
- Spiritual Inspiration: Catholics draw spiritual inspiration from Mary's faith and her cooperation with God's plan.

The connection between Mary and the Old Testament offers a profound tapestry of theological insights, typology, and spiritual inspiration for Catholics. It underscores Mary's unique and central role in God's plan of salvation and invites believers to contemplate her example of faith, obedience, and humility as they navigate their own faith journeys.

Chapter 10: Applying the Old Testament to Catholic Life

As we journey through the pages of the Old Testament, we encounter a wealth of stories, teachings, prophecies, and wisdom that have shaped the foundations of the Catholic faith. While the Old Testament may be a collection of ancient texts, its relevance to the lives of Catholics today remains strikingly profound. The Old Testament is a living word that continues to speak to Catholics in their contemporary contexts. It offers timeless lessons, moral guidance, and spiritual insights that are invaluable for navigating the challenges and joys of life.

1. Moral and Ethical Guidance

The Old Testament provides a robust framework for moral and ethical decision-making. Through the commandments, laws, and teachings found within its pages, Catholics discover principles that guide them in making choices that align with their faith and values. These moral teachings are as relevant today as they were in ancient times, offering a compass for living virtuous lives.

2. Spiritual Enrichment

The Old Testament is a treasure trove of spiritual wisdom and practices. Catholics can draw from the psalms, prayers, and examples of faith found in these texts to deepen their relationship with God. The rich tapestry of spiritual experiences, from the psalmist's heartfelt cries to the prophets' visions of God's glory, invites believers to explore the depths of their own spirituality.

3. Lessons from Biblical Figures

The Old Testament introduces readers to a diverse array of biblical figures, each with their own strengths, weaknesses, and lessons to offer. From the faith of Abraham and the wisdom of Solomon to the courage of Esther and the repentance of King David, these characters provide valuable insights into human nature and the possibilities of divine transformation.

4. Theological Reflection

The theological themes woven throughout the Old Testament continue to inform Catholic theology and doctrine. Concepts such as covenant, redemption, justice, and God's providence find their roots in these ancient texts. By delving into the Old Testament, Catholics gain a deeper understanding of the theological foundations of their faith.

5. A Source of Hope and Comfort

In times of trials, tribulations, and uncertainty, the Old Testament offers stories of hope, resilience, and God's unfailing presence. The narratives of the Israelites' journey through the wilderness, the prophets' messages of restoration, and the promises of a Messiah provide comfort and assurance to Catholics facing life's challenges.

This chapter will explore practical ways in which Catholics can apply the wisdom of the Old Testament to their daily lives. Whether in matters of family, work, relationships, or personal growth, the Old Testament serves as a guide for navigating life's complexities while remaining faithful to the teachings of the Catholic Church.

The Old Testament is a living testament to God's enduring presence and guidance. As Catholics, we are called to immerse ourselves in these sacred texts, to reflect on their significance, and to apply their wisdom to our lives. In doing so, we draw closer to the heart of our faith, finding strength, inspiration, and a deeper connection to God through the timeless words of the Old Testament.

Old Testament Values and Ethics

The Old Testament is a rich source of moral and ethical guidance that continues to hold relevance in the lives of Catholics today. Its teachings, principles, and stories provide a foundation for understanding and applying key values and ethics in various aspects of life.

1. Monotheism and Worship of God

The Old Testament firmly establishes the belief in one God, Yahweh, as the foundational tenet of faith. The First Commandment, "You shall have no other gods before me, (NIV)" underscores the exclusive worship of God. Catholics are reminded of the importance of monotheism and the need to prioritize their relationship with God above all else.

2. Covenant and Loyalty

The concept of covenant is central to the Old Testament, highlighting the sacred agreements between God and His people. The fidelity and loyalty demonstrated in these covenants serve as a model for Catholics in their relationships with God and one another. Upholding promises and commitments is a core ethical value derived from the Old Testament.

3. Justice and Compassion

The Old Testament is replete with teachings on justice and compassion. The prophets, in particular, championed the cause of the oppressed and called for social justice. Catholics are called to emulate these values by advocating for the marginalized and ensuring fairness and equity in society.

4. Mercy and Forgiveness

The Old Testament showcases God's abundant mercy and willingness to forgive even in the face of human frailty and sin. The story of King David's repentance and the prodigal son's return are emblematic of God's compassionate nature. Catholics are encouraged to extend forgiveness and show mercy to others, mirroring God's own disposition.

5. Respect for Human Dignity

The Old Testament teaches the inherent dignity of every human being as they are created in the image of God. This foundational principle underpins the Catholic Church's teachings on the sanctity of life, the dignity of the human person, and the importance of treating others with respect, regardless of their background or circumstances.

6. Charity and Almsgiving

The Old Testament emphasizes the importance of charity and almsgiving as acts of kindness and generosity toward those in need. The practice of tithing and giving to the poor reflects the Old Testament's ethical imperative to share blessings with others. Catholics are encouraged to continue these practices in their commitment to helping those less fortunate.

7. Honesty and Integrity

The Old Testament consistently condemns dishonesty, fraud, and deceit. The Eighth Commandment, "You shall not bear false witness," underscores the importance of truthfulness and integrity. Catholics are called to be honest and forthright in their dealings with others.

8. Humility and Obedience

The stories of biblical figures like Moses, who exhibited humility and obedience to God's commands, serve as examples for Catholics. Humility, recognizing one's dependence on

God, and obedience to God's will are esteemed virtues within the Catholic moral framework.

9. Gratitude and Thanksgiving

The Old Testament contains numerous psalms and passages that exhort believers to offer thanks and praise to God. Gratitude is seen as an essential aspect of the Christian life, reminding Catholics to acknowledge God's blessings and providence.

10. Stewardship of Creation

The Old Testament teaches that humanity is entrusted with the care of God's creation. Catholics are called to be responsible stewards of the environment, respecting the earth's resources and taking measures to protect and preserve the planet for future generations.

Old Testament values and ethics serve as the bedrock of Catholic moral theology. They provide a moral framework that informs decisions, actions, and interactions, helping Catholics to live out their faith authentically and in accordance with God's plan. By drawing upon the ethical wisdom of the Old Testament, Catholics strengthen their commitment to living virtuous lives and contributing positively to society.

The Old Testament in Catholic Liturgy

The Old Testament plays a significant role in the liturgical life of the Catholic Church. It is woven into the fabric of the Mass, the liturgical seasons, and the sacraments, serving as a constant reminder of the rich heritage and continuity between the Old and New Testaments.

1. Liturgical Readings

One of the most prominent ways in which the Old Testament is integrated into Catholic worship is through the reading of sacred texts during the liturgy. The Old Testament readings, along with those from the New Testament and the Gospel, are an essential component of the Mass. These readings are selected according to the liturgical calendar and often reflect the themes of the day or season.

- First Reading: The Old Testament reading typically occurs immediately after the Responsorial Psalm and before the New Testament reading. It provides an opportunity for Catholics to hear and reflect on passages from books such as Genesis, Exodus, Isaiah, and the Psalms, among others.
- Seasonal Emphasis: The Old Testament readings are carefully chosen to align with the liturgical season. For example, during Advent, the Old Testament readings frequently focus on prophecies related to the coming of the Messiah, while Lent often features passages highlighting God's mercy and covenant.

2. Responsorial Psalms

The Psalms, a collection of poetic and prayerful verses from the Old Testament, are an integral part of the Mass. The Responsorial Psalm, sung or recited after the First Reading, is often drawn from the Book of Psalms. These psalms serve as a liturgical response to the preceding reading, allowing the congregation to engage actively in worship.

- Liturgical Themes: The Responsorial Psalms enhance the liturgical themes of the day and provide a way for Catholics to express praise, petition, and thanksgiving in response to the Word of God.

3. Feasts and Solemnities

Various liturgical feasts and solemnities throughout the Catholic calendar have their origins in the Old Testament. For example:

- Feast of the Presentation of the Lord: This feast commemorates the presentation of the infant Jesus in the Temple, as prescribed in the Old Testament law (Luke 2:22-38).
- Holy Thursday: The institution of the Eucharist during the Last Supper is rooted in the Old Testament Passover meal.
- Easter Vigil: The liturgy of the Easter Vigil draws extensively from the Old Testament, recounting salvation history through readings, psalms, and prayers.

4. Sacraments and Rites

The Old Testament also influences the celebration of the sacraments and other liturgical rites within the Catholic Church:

- Baptism: The biblical motif of water as a symbol of purification and renewal is drawn from the Old Testament, particularly the crossing of the Red Sea (Exodus 14) and the cleansing rituals described in Leviticus.
- Confirmation: The anointing with sacred chrism during Confirmation traces its origins to the anointing of priests and kings in the Old Testament.
- Matrimony: The Old Testament's portrayal of marriage as a covenant between God and His people informs the Catholic understanding of the sacrament of Matrimony.

5. Lectionary and Liturgical Calendar

The Catholic Church follows a liturgical calendar that cycles through different seasons, each with its own set of readings and themes. The Old Testament readings are integrated into this calendar, allowing Catholics to journey through salvation history and the life of Christ in a structured and cyclical manner.

The Old Testament's presence in Catholic liturgy is a living testament to the continuity of God's plan of salvation. It underscores the unity of the Old and New Testaments, reinforcing the belief that the entirety of Scripture points to Jesus Christ as the fulfillment of God's promises. Through its inclusion in liturgical celebrations, the Old Testament enriches the worship experience of Catholics, connecting them with the faith of their ancestors and guiding them in their journey of faith and discipleship.

Studying and Reading the Old Testament Today

In the modern world, the Old Testament remains a vital and relevant part of Catholic faith and spirituality. Studying and reading the Old Testament today is an exploration of ancient texts and a vibrant encounter with the living Word of God.

1. Sacred Scripture in the Digital Age

In today's digital age, the Old Testament is more accessible than ever before. Catholics can access multiple translations, commentaries, and study tools online, making it easier to explore the texts and their interpretations. Online resources, apps, and websites dedicated to Scripture study offer a wealth of information, facilitating both personal and communal engagement with the Old Testament.

2. Choosing a Bible Translation

Selecting an appropriate Bible translation is crucial for effective Old Testament study. The choice of translation should align with the reader's preferences, understanding, and spiritual needs. Common translations used by Catholics include the New American Bible (NAB), the Revised Standard Version Catholic Edition (RSV-CE), and the Douay-Rheims Bible.

3. Study Bibles and Commentaries

For those seeking a deeper understanding of the Old Testament, study Bibles and commentaries are invaluable resources. These books provide explanations, historical context, and theological insights that enhance the reading experience. Examples of study Bibles for Catholics include the Catholic Study Bible and the Ignatius Catholic Study Bible series.

4. Daily Scripture Reading

Incorporating daily Scripture reading into one's routine is a powerful way to engage with the Old Testament. The Catholic Church encourages the faithful to read and meditate on the Word of God regularly. Daily devotionals and reading plans can guide individuals through selected Old Testament passages, fostering spiritual growth and reflection.

5. Joining Scripture Study Groups

Many Catholic parishes and communities offer Scripture study groups that gather to explore and discuss the Old Testament together. Joining such groups can provide valuable insights, shared perspectives, and a sense of community as participants journey through the Old Testament.

6. Lectio Divina

Lectio Divina, a centuries-old Christian practice, involves a prayerful and meditative reading of Scripture. Catholics can apply Lectio Divina to the Old Testament, allowing the texts to speak to their hearts, deepening their relationship with God, and nurturing a contemplative approach to Scripture.

7. Exploring Key Old Testament Themes

To gain a comprehensive understanding of the Old Testament, it is helpful to explore key themes and narratives. These themes include covenant, salvation history, prophecy, the Messiah, and the journey of God's people. Focusing on these overarching concepts illuminates the Old Testament's unity and its connection to the New Testament.

8. Resources for Understanding Hebrew Scriptures

For those interested in a more scholarly approach to the Old Testament, resources for understanding Hebrew Scriptures can be valuable. Courses, books, and online materials provide insights into the original language, culture, and historical context of the Old Testament, enriching one's study.

9. Praying with the Old Testament

Prayer is an integral part of reading the Old Testament. Catholics can use Old Testament passages as sources of inspiration for personal prayer, reflection, and meditation. The Psalms, in particular, offer a rich reservoir of prayers and praises that resonate with human experiences and emotions.

10. Theological Reflection and Application

Studying and reading the Old Testament should not be an academic exercise alone; it should lead to theological reflection and practical application. Catholics are encouraged to consider how the Old Testament's teachings, values, and stories can inform their beliefs, values, and actions in daily life.

Studying and reading the Old Testament today is an integral part of Catholic faith formation and spiritual growth. It strengthens the foundation of belief, deepens the connection to the Church's rich tradition, and enriches the Catholic experience of encountering God through His Word. Whether through personal reading, group study, or guided reflection, the Old Testament continues to inspire, challenge, and guide Catholics on their faith journey.

Conclusion and Further Exploration

As we reach the final chapter of "The Catholic Old Testament: A Beginner's Guide," we find ourselves at a juncture of both culmination and commencement. Our journey through the Old Testament has been one of discovery, illumination, and faith enrichment. We've delved into the historical and cultural contexts, explored the literary styles, and uncovered the key themes and messages that make the Old Testament a living testament to God's enduring love and providence. We've witnessed the unfolding of salvation history, encountered the lives of biblical figures, and grappled with profound theological questions.

As we conclude our exploration, it is essential to recognize that the study of the Old Testament is not a finite endeavor. Instead, it marks the beginning of a lifelong engagement with God's Word. The lessons, values, and insights gleaned from the Old Testament are meant to inform and shape our beliefs, actions, and relationships as Catholics.

In this chapter, we encourage readers to embark on a journey of further exploration:

1. Lifelong Learning

Studying the Old Testament is a lifelong pursuit. It involves a commitment to continuous learning and growth in faith. As we conclude this guide, we invite you to delve deeper into specific Old Testament books, themes, or figures that resonate with your spiritual journey.

2. Bible Study Groups

Consider joining or forming a Bible study group within your parish or community. These groups provide opportunities for communal exploration, shared insights, and vibrant discussions that can deepen your understanding of the Old Testament.

3. Retreats and Workshops

Participating in retreats or workshops focused on the Old Testament can be a transformative experience. These events offer guidance, reflection, and spiritual renewal, fostering a deeper connection to Scripture.

4. Exploring Jewish Roots

Understanding the Jewish roots of the Old Testament can provide valuable insights into the context and culture in which these texts were written. Explore resources and engage in dialogue with Jewish scholars to gain a broader perspective.

5. Applying Old Testament Wisdom

Take the lessons learned from the Old Testament and apply them to your daily life. Consider how the values, ethics, and moral teachings can shape your decisions, interactions, and relationships.

6. Praying with Scripture

Continue to incorporate Old Testament passages into your daily prayer life. The Psalms, in particular, offer a wealth of prayers and praises that can enrich your spiritual journey.

7. Engaging with Catholic Theology

Deepen your understanding of Catholic theology by exploring how Old Testament themes and concepts continue to inform and shape the Church's teachings and doctrines.

As we conclude this guide, we hope you embark on a continuing journey of faith that is informed and inspired by the Old Testament. May the wisdom, stories, and teachings of this sacred scripture continue to illuminate your path, strengthen your faith, and draw you closer to the God who reveals Himself through its pages.

The Old Testament is an open invitation—a source of ongoing revelation and exploration. In the words of the psalmist, "Your word is a lamp to my feet and a light to my path" (Psalm 119:105, NIV). May your journey with the Old Testament be filled with illumination, inspiration, and a deepening of your Catholic faith.

The Ongoing Relevance of the Old Testament

In the modern world, with its fast-paced changes and evolving belief systems, the Old Testament continues to maintain its enduring relevance in the lives of Catholics. Despite its ancient origins and cultural contexts, the Old Testament holds a special place within the Catholic faith.

1. Foundation of Christian Faith

The Old Testament forms the foundation upon which the Christian faith stands. It is the precursor to the New Testament, setting the stage for the coming of Jesus Christ. Catholics recognize that the promises, prophecies, and covenants of the Old Testament find their fulfillment in Christ, emphasizing the inseparable connection between the two testaments.

2. Enduring Moral and Ethical Guidance

The moral and ethical teachings found in the Old Testament continue to resonate with Catholics today. Principles such as the Ten Commandments, love of neighbor, justice, and compassion provide timeless guidance for navigating the complexities of contemporary life. Catholics turn to these teachings for ethical direction in a world often marked by moral ambiguity.

3. Reflection of Human Experience

The Old Testament reflects the breadth and depth of the human experience. Its stories encompass joy and sorrow, triumph and failure, faithfulness and betrayal. These narratives are not distant tales but mirrors of the human condition, offering solace and understanding to those grappling with life's challenges.

4. Inspiration for Worship and Devotion

The Psalms, a collection of poetic and prayerful verses from the Old Testament, continue to inspire Catholic worship and devotion. The emotional depth and spiritual richness of the Psalms provide a means for Catholics to express their deepest feelings, whether in times of joy, sorrow, praise, or lament.

5. Lessons from Biblical Figures

The lives of biblical figures in the Old Testament serve as sources of inspiration and guidance. From Abraham's faithfulness to David's repentance, these figures exemplify virtues and offer valuable lessons for Catholics striving to live out their faith authentically.

6. Theological Foundations

Many foundational theological concepts within Catholicism, such as covenant, redemption, and God's providence, are rooted in the Old Testament. An understanding of these concepts deepens Catholics' appreciation of their faith and their connection to the broader tradition of the Church.

7. Challenges and Comfort in Adversity

The Old Testament narratives provide both challenges and comfort. They challenge Catholics to confront their own shortcomings and call them to a life of virtue. Simultaneously, stories of God's deliverance, restoration, and faithfulness offer comfort and hope, especially in times of adversity and suffering.

8. A Source of Dialogue and Interpretation

The Old Testament invites ongoing dialogue and interpretation. Catholics engage in the dynamic process of reading, studying, and reflecting upon these sacred texts. Interpretation adapts to changing contexts and theological challenges, ensuring the continued relevance and applicability of the Old Testament.

9. Spiritual Depth and Transformation

Reading and meditating upon the Old Testament texts can lead to profound spiritual depth and transformation. The timeless truths contained within these pages challenge Catholics to grow in faith, develop a deeper relationship with God, and live out their beliefs more fully.

10. A Living Word

Above all, the Old Testament is a living word—a divine revelation that speaks directly to the hearts and lives of Catholics. Its messages challenge, comfort, inspire, and transform, continuing to shape the faith and spirituality of those who encounter its timeless wisdom.

The ongoing relevance of the Old Testament within the Catholic faith underscores its status as a living and enduring scripture. Catholics find in these ancient texts a source of guidance, inspiration, and spiritual nourishment that enriches their relationship with God and deepens their commitment to living out the values and teachings of their faith. The Old Testament remains a timeless testament to God's enduring presence, love, and providence in the lives of believers.

Recommended Resources for Deeper Study

As you embark on your journey of exploring the Old Testament within the Catholic faith, you may find it beneficial to delve deeper into specific aspects of these sacred scriptures. Fortunately, there are numerous resources available to assist you in your pursuit of deeper understanding and engagement.

Books for In-Depth Study:

- "The Catholic Study Bible" - Edited by Donald Senior, John Collins, and Mary Ann Getty, this comprehensive study Bible includes extensive commentary, historical background, and theological insights.
- "A Catholic Introduction to the Bible: The Old Testament" - By Brant Pitre, John Bergsma, this book offers a scholarly yet accessible overview of the Old Testament.
- "Introduction to the Hebrew Bible" - By John J. Collins, this book provides a thorough introduction to the Old Testament, offering historical, literary, and theological analysis.
- "The Navarre Bible" - This series of books provides both the text and commentary on each book of the Bible, offering a detailed Catholic perspective.
- "The Jewish Study Bible" - Edited by Adele Berlin and Marc Zvi Brettler, this resource provides insights from Jewish scholars on the Old Testament, offering a broader perspective.

Online Resources:

- Bible Gateway (biblegateway.com) - This website offers access to multiple Bible translations, commentaries, and reading plans.
- United States Conference of Catholic Bishops (usccb.org) - The USCCB website provides access to the New American Bible (NAB) translation and offers resources for reading and studying the Old Testament.
- Catholic Bible Online (catholicbible.online) - This website provides a free online Catholic Bible with footnotes and cross-references.

- Catholic Answers (catholic.com) - Catholic Answers offers articles, videos, and podcasts on various topics related to the Catholic faith, including the Old Testament.

Courses and Seminars:

- Local Parishes and Dioceses - Many local Catholic parishes and dioceses offer Bible study courses and seminars, providing an opportunity for communal learning and discussion.
- Online Learning Platforms - Websites like Udemy, Coursera, and edX offer courses on the Old Testament and related topics. You can explore courses from renowned universities and institutions.
- Catholic Theological Schools - Consider enrolling in courses or seminars at Catholic theological schools or seminaries in your area. These institutions often offer specialized courses on Scripture.

Organizations and Associations:

- The Catholic Biblical Association of America (catholicbiblical.org) - This organization promotes scholarly study of the Bible and offers resources for biblical research and education.
- The Society of Biblical Literature (sbl-site.org) - While not Catholic-specific, this organization is a valuable resource for biblical scholars and students.
- The Augustine Institute (augustineinstitute.org) - This Catholic institution offers various resources, including online courses and Bible studies.

Libraries and Academic Institutions:

- University Libraries - Local universities often have extensive libraries with academic resources, including scholarly journals, books, and research materials related to the Old Testament.

- Seminaries and Theological Libraries - Some seminaries and theological institutions allow public access to their libraries, providing a wealth of theological and biblical resources.

Joining Bible Study Groups:

Consider joining or forming a Bible study group within your parish or community. Engaging in group discussions and sharing insights can deepen your understanding of the Old Testament.

Engaging with Jewish Scholars:

Exploring the Old Testament from a Jewish perspective can offer unique insights. Consider engaging in dialogue or reading materials authored by Jewish scholars who specialize in the Hebrew Bible.

These recommended resources are just a starting point for your journey into the Old Testament. Depending on your specific interests and goals, you may find certain resources more appealing or relevant than others. Whether you choose to read scholarly books, participate in online courses, or engage in communal Bible study, your pursuit of deeper understanding will enrich your faith and spiritual journey within the Catholic tradition.

Appendices

A. Glossary of Terms

This glossary provides definitions for key terms and concepts related to the study of the Old Testament within the Catholic tradition. As you explore "The Catholic Old Testament: A Beginner's Guide," refer to this glossary to enhance your understanding of the subject matter.

1. *Abraham*: The patriarch and father of the Abrahamic covenant, a central figure in the Old Testament. God promised Abraham numerous descendants and a land, a covenant that laid the foundation for the people of Israel.

2. *Covenant*: A sacred agreement or contract between God and His people. The Old Testament features several significant covenants, including the Abrahamic, Mosaic, and Davidic covenants.

3. *Exodus*: The central event in the Old Testament in which God liberated the Israelites from slavery in Egypt, led by the prophet Moses. It marks the beginning of their journey to the Promised Land.

4. *Israelites*: The descendants of Jacob (also known as Israel) and the people chosen by God to be in a covenant relationship with Him. They are often referred to as the "Children of Israel" or "Hebrews."

5. *Judges*: Leaders and military deliverers chosen by God to guide the Israelites during times of crisis and apostasy. The period of the Judges is described in the Book of Judges.

6. *Moses*: A central figure in the Old Testament who received the Ten Commandments from God on Mount Sinai and led the Israelites out of Egypt during the Exodus.

7. *Psalms*: A collection of religious songs and prayers found in the Book of Psalms. They are used in worship, devotion, and personal reflection and are often attributed to King David.

8. *Prophets*: Individuals chosen by God to deliver His messages and warnings to the people of Israel. The Old Testament contains both major and minor prophets, including Isaiah, Jeremiah, and Ezekiel.

9. *Salvation History*: The narrative of God's plan for the redemption and salvation of humanity. It unfolds throughout the Old and New Testaments, culminating in the life, death, and resurrection of Jesus Christ.

10. *Tabernacle*: A portable sanctuary used by the Israelites during their wilderness journey. It served as the dwelling place of God's presence and a central place of worship.

11. *Ten Commandments*: A foundational set of moral and ethical principles given by God to Moses on Mount Sinai. They are a guide for living a just and righteous life.

12. *Torah*: The first five books of the Old Testament, also known as the Pentateuch. They include Genesis, Exodus, Leviticus, Numbers, and Deuteronomy and contain laws, history, and religious teachings.

13. *Yahweh*: The sacred name of God as revealed to Moses at the burning bush. It is often translated as "I Am Who I Am" and is considered the personal name of the God of Israel.

14. *Zion*: A prominent biblical term often used to refer to the city of Jerusalem or the spiritual center of Israel. It has a strong connection to God's presence.

15. *Exegesis*: The process of interpreting and understanding biblical texts, taking into account their historical, cultural, and literary contexts.

16. *Theology*: The study of God and religious beliefs, including the systematic exploration of religious doctrine and teachings within the Catholic tradition.

17. *Inspiration of Scripture*: The belief that the Bible is divinely inspired, with its authors guided by the Holy Spirit to communicate God's message.

18. *Sacred Tradition*: The unwritten teachings and practices of the Catholic Church, complementing the Scriptures as sources of faith and doctrine.

19. *Canon*: The official list of books recognized as divinely inspired and authoritative for the Catholic faith. 46 books make up the canon of the Old Testament.

20. *Catholic Biblical Interpretation*: The approach to interpreting the Bible within the Catholic tradition, guided by the teachings of the Church and a commitment to understanding the Scriptures in their fullness.

B. Timeline of Old Testament Events

This timeline provides an overview of key events and figures in the Old Testament, highlighting significant moments in the history of the people of Israel within the Catholic tradition. Refer to this timeline while reading "The Catholic Old Testament: A Beginner's Guide" to better understand the historical context of the Old Testament narrative.

Pre-Old Testament Period:

- c. 2000-1800 BCE: The patriarch Abraham is called by God and enters into a covenant with Him.
- c. 1800-1600 BCE: The patriarch Isaac and his son Jacob continue the covenantal lineage.
- c. 1600-1500 BCE: Jacob's descendants, the Israelites, migrate to Egypt during a famine.

Exodus and Early History:

- c. 1250 BCE: The Exodus from Egypt under the leadership of Moses.
- c. 1250-1220 BCE: The Israelites wander in the wilderness for 40 years.
- c. 1250-1200 BCE: The giving of the Ten Commandments on Mount Sinai.
- c. 1200-1025 BCE: The period of the Judges, with leaders such as Deborah, Gideon, and Samson.
- c. 1025-922 BCE: The establishment of the Israelite monarchy with King Saul, followed by King David and King Solomon.

Divided Kingdom and Prophets:

- c. 922 BCE: The division of the united kingdom into the northern kingdom of Israel (with its capital in Samaria) and the southern kingdom of Judah (with its capital in Jerusalem).
- c. 750-700 BCE: The ministry of the prophets, including Isaiah, Jeremiah, and Hosea, who called the people to repentance.
- 722 BCE: The fall of the northern kingdom of Israel to the Assyrians.
- 586 BCE: The destruction of the southern kingdom of Judah and the First Temple in Jerusalem by the Babylonians.

Exile and Return:

- 587-538 BCE: The Babylonian Exile, during which the Israelites were taken captive to Babylon.
- 539 BCE: The Persian king Cyrus the Great allows the Israelites to return to their homeland and rebuild the Second Temple in Jerusalem.
- 516 BCE: The Second Temple's completion.
- c. 450-400 BCE: The compilation of the Torah (the first five books of the Old Testament) and the prophetic books.

- c. 330-300 BCE: The translation of the Hebrew Bible into Greek, known as the Septuagint.

Hellenistic and Roman Periods:

- c. 332 BCE: The conquest of Israel by Alexander the Great and the spread of Hellenistic culture.
- c. 167-160 BCE: The Maccabean Revolt and the purification of the Second Temple (celebrated during Hanukkah).
- 63 BCE: The Roman general Pompey captures Jerusalem, leading to Roman rule over Judea.
- 4 BCE - 30 CE: The life and ministry of Jesus Christ, whose teachings and message are recorded in the New Testament.

The Old Testament Texts:

- c. 5th to 2nd centuries BCE: The writing, editing, and compilation of various Old Testament books, including historical, prophetic, and wisdom literature.
- 1st century CE: The Old Testament texts are preserved and revered within the Jewish and early Christian communities.

This timeline offers a chronological framework for the events and periods covered in the Old Testament. It serves as a valuable reference point for understanding the historical context of the Old Testament narrative and its significance within the Catholic tradition.

THANK YOU FOR READING!

If you've read "The Catholic Old Testament: A Beginner's Guide" and found it informative and helpful in your journey to understanding the Old Testament within the Catholic tradition, we invite you to share your thoughts with others by leaving a review on Amazon. Your feedback can make a significant difference in helping fellow readers discover this valuable resource.

Please consider taking a few minutes to write an honest review and share your insights, whether you appreciated the clarity of the content, the depth of the explanations, or the relevance of the topics discussed. Your review can help prospective readers make an informed decision and benefit from this beginner's guide.

Your feedback is greatly appreciated, and we look forward to hearing your thoughts on "The Catholic Old Testament: A Beginner's Guide." Thank you for your support!

All photos are from Unsplash.com.

Printed in Great Britain
by Amazon